Fellowship

A DEVOTIONAL STUDY OF THE EPISTLES OF JOHN

by John G. Mitchell

MULTNOMAH PRESS
PORTLAND, OREGON 97266

Also by John G. Mitchell:
  An Everlasting Love: A Devotional Study of the Gospel of John
  Bible Study: The Basis of Christian Growth

Scripture references in this volume are from the King James Version of
the Bible.

FELLOWSHIP
© 1974 by Multnomah Press
Portland, Oregon 97266

Printed in the United States of America

Library of Congress Cataloging in Publication Data

Mitchell, John G.,   1892-
  Fellowship: a devotional study of the epistles of John.

  1. Bible. N.T. Epistles of John—Commentaries.
I. Title
BS2805.3.M49   1984   227'.9406   84-1938
ISBN 0-930014-06-5 (pbk.)

              86   87   88   89   90   –   12   11   10   9   8   7

CONTENTS

FOREWORD

Those who have enjoyed the public ministry of Dr. John G. Mitchell in the pulpit, classroom, and his radio broadcasts have profited greatly by his warm and penetrating expositions of the Word of God. To an unusual degree, Dr. Mitchell has the gift of making the Word of God practical and relating it to the believer's walk with his Saviour.

The same intimate and stimulating ministry which has characterized his teaching is captured in this exposition of the Epistle of John. By nature of its contents, The Epistle of John is addressed to the family of God. Although containing many important theological truths, the emphasis in this epistle is on the practical application of it to the walk of the believer. This epistle is unusually suited to express the main thrust of Dr. Mitchell's effective ministry, as he has preached the gospel for more than fifty years.

Many preachers of the Word who are successful in the pulpit become lifeless when their words are reduced to writing. Dr. Mitchell is the exception to this rule. His exposition of this epistle has the same warm touch which characterizes his public ministry. Readers will find their hearts blessed, their souls encouraged, and their minds instructed by the truth of God.

Any exposition of the Epistle of John has unusual problems because its structure is not organized theologically in the same way that is true of the Epistle of the Romans. A suitable outline of the First Epistle of John has often puzzled expositors. Dr. Mitchell has surmounted this problem, and his exposition of this epistle flows smoothly from one theme to the next, reflecting the maturity of years of study and rich spiritual experience on the part of the one giving the exposition.

Accordingly, it is a genuine pleasure to recommend this exposition to all who want to know more of the marvelous revelation presented in this inspired book of the Bible.

John F. Walvoord
President, Dallas Theological Seminary

PREFACE

These messages were given on the radio program "Know Your Bible Hour," and many have asked that they be printed. The teacher has gleaned from many sources and only desires that the children of God should know the Lord to whom they have been joined, and have daily fellowship with Him.

It is wonderful to know we can have fellowship with God who is Light, 2:5; with God who is Righteous, 2:29, 3:7; and with God who is Love, 4:8,16. What a privilege and what a joy the believer can have in fellowship with Him.

I am very grateful to Dr. Dorothy Ritzmann and my wife, Mary Mitchell, for the many hours they have spent in editing this brief series of messages. This book would not have been written without their help and encouragement. I am sure the Lord will richly bless them for all the time they have spent in this ministry.

THE JOY OF FELLOWSHIP

The heart of God yearns for the fellowship of His people. We hear men speak of how we ought to have fellowship with God, and rightly so. But do we ever think that the Lord yearns and longs for our fellowship? This was why God created man, but man failed God. This was why God redeemed sinners, in order that He might have someone with whom He can have fellowship.

In Amos 3:3 we read, "How can two walk together unless they have an appointment?" We who are believers in the Lord Jesus Christ have an appointment with God and God has an appointment with us. God always keeps His appointments. We are the ones who do not keep the appointment with God.

Adam and Eve had an appointment with God. "And they heard the voice of the Lord God walking in the garden in the cool of the day: and Adam and his wife hid themselves from the presence of the Lord God amongst the trees of the garden. And the Lord God called unto Adam, and said unto him, Where art thou?" (Genesis 3:8). Sin did not keep God from the appointment, but it did keep Adam from it. We have an appointment with God, and sin keeps us from meeting with God.

This truth is all through the Bible. God wants our fellowship. He found fellowship with Enoch, a man who lived in an ungodly world. He found Noah, who lived in a violent world. Then He found Abraham who lived in an idolatrous, corrupt world (cp. Romans 1). Note how God enjoyed His fellowship with Abraham. He is called the friend of God in II Chronicles 20:7, "Art not Thou our God". . . you gave this land "to the seed of Abraham thy friend forever," and in Isaiah 41:8, "The seed of Abraham *my* friend" (cp. Genesis 18:17).

Exodus 33:11 reveals that God enjoyed intimate friendship with Moses, who lived among a stiff-necked, murmuring people, "And the Lord spoke unto Moses face to face, as a man speaketh unto his friend." This is restated in Deuteronomy 34:10, "Moses, whom the Lord knew face to face."

Such fellowship has ever been the desire of the Lord from the beginning. Even our Lord expressed it to His disciples in John 15:15, "Henceforth, I call you not servants; for the servant knoweth not what his Lord doeth; but I have called you friends; for all things that I have heard of my Father, I have made known unto you." This is not only relationship, but intimacy of fellowship. It is the great desire of the heart of God that we should know something of how He wants our fellowship.

This is the heartbeat of the Epistles of John. In chapter 1:3-4, "Truly our fellowship (partnership) is with the Father and with His Son Jesus Christ. And these things write we unto you, that your joy may be full."

May our Lord by His Spirit, through His Word make this very real to you, personally and individually, and may He bring you unto Himself in such sweet fellowship. What does He desire? Our fellowship.

THE FIRST
EPISTLE
GENERAL
OF JOHN

The Epistle of John was written approximately twenty-five years after Paul had written his prison Epistles. According to the historian Clement, it was after John had returned from the Isle of Patmos, where he had written the Book of Revelation, that he wrote the Epistle of John. He had been set at liberty from his slavery by the Romans and had gone to Ephesus. While in Ephesus, the aged John wrote this precious letter.

If Dr. Westcott, the great British Greek scholar, is correct (and I believe he is), the First Epistle of John is the last of the New Testament writings. Considering this, it is interesting to compare the first verse of Genesis, "In the beginning God," with the last two verses written in the Epistle of John: ". . . that we may know him that is true, and we are in him that is true, even in his Son Jesus Christ. This is the true God, and eternal life. Little children, keep yourselves from idols. Amen."

One of the reasons for the writing of this Epistle was that John might warn against a heresy which had sprung up in the early church. It was called the Gnostic heresy. The Gnostics denied the incarnation. They did not believe that God could be manifest in human flesh. They said that matter is evil and it was unthinkable to them that a holy God could take the form of man.

In his answer to the Gnostics, John declares emphatically that there can be no spiritual life, no fellowship or relationship with God, apart from the Incarnate Word of God. In his declaration, he carries us into the glorious heights of the marvellous revelation of God in Christ. He makes it very clear that the yearning of his own heart and the yearning of the heart of God is that every redeemed child of His might enjoy to the full an intimate fellowship with God. This fellowship is to be found through relationship with the Incarnate Word of God. This, then, is the emphasis of this Epistle. Here we have the truth concerning the Incarnate Word and the blessed privilege of our fellowship with Him.

RELATION OF THE EPISTLE OF JOHN
TO THE NEW TESTAMENT

In every book of the New Testament the person of Jesus Christ is pre-eminent! The first four books of the New Testament are the four Gospels in which we find the wonderful story of the coming of our Saviour into the world and His life here for thirty-three and a half years. The Acts of the Apostles is the history of the beginning of His church. The Epistles have to do with doctrine and instruction. There are three authors of the Epistles:

Paul, the Apostle of faith,

Peter, the Apostle of hope,

John, the Apostle of love.

The New Testament concludes with the Book of the Revelation which gives to us the prophecy of the last days and the return of the Lord.

Let us now briefly compare John's Gospel with his Epistle. In the Gospel of John we read: "For God so loved the world, that he gave his only begotten Son, that whosoever believeth in him should not perish, but have everlasting life" (John 3:16). In the Epistle of John this is restated: "Herein is love, not that we loved God, but that he loved us, and sent his Son to be the propitiation for our sins" (I John 4:10), and, "Hereby perceive we the love of

God, because he laid down his life for us: and we ought to lay down our lives for the brethren" (I John 3:16). Thus the Epistle of John *reinforces the basic gospel truth* as it is set forth in the Gospel of John.

The Gospel of John gives us the fulfillment of Isaiah 40:9, "Say unto the cities of Judah, Behold your God!" In the Gospel, He is made flesh to dwell among us and we have our relationship with Him. The important truth in the Gospel of John is that we have life in and through the Son of God. "In him was life" (John 1:4). The Gospel tells us that we *receive* eternal life by faith in the Lord Jesus Christ when we accept Him into our life as our own personal Saviour. The Epistle shows us how we are to *enjoy* that life in Christ.

In the Gospel, we *have* life because God *declares* it and we receive it by faith. In the Epistle, we *know* we have eternal life because we *experience* it. In the Gospel of John, eternal life is manifested in the *Son of God;* in the Epistle of John life is manifested in the *children of God.* In the Gospel, we find that life can come only through *relationship* with Jesus Christ, the Incarnate Word of God. In the Epistle, we cannot have *fellowship* with God apart from the Incarnate Word of God.

We stress that both relationship and fellowship are dependent on the Incarnate Word of God. Heresies of the present day declare Christ to be a mere man, a good man, and a wonderful teacher, but not God Incarnate. This we must refute.

It is also interesting to compare the Book of Hebrews with this Epistle of John. Hebrews shows God in His *governmental* dealings with His people. In Hebrews, we are "outside the camp" (Heb. 13:11) in our relationship to the world but "within the veil" (Heb. 6:19; 10:19-22) in our relationship to God. We have access into the presence of God.

The Epistle of John sets forth the relationship in the *family* of God. In John's Epistle, we not only enter into the Holy of Holies, into heaven itself, but we have fellowship with the God who is there! This is the amazing truth! We, who are created beings, members of the human family, born in sin, rebels against God, can be redeemed, born again, become recipients of His life in us, and be brought into such a relationship with God that we can come with boldness to the very throne of God. Not only this, but also we can have intimate, blessed fellowship with the One who is on the throne. This is the unspeakable glorious truth of the First Epistle of John

THE THEME OF THE FIRST EPISTLE OF JOHN

That which we have seen and heard declare we unto you, that ye also may have fellowship with us: and truly our fellowship is with the Father, and with his Son Jesus Christ (I John 1:3).

In this Epistle we have the wonderful truth concerning the family of God. The word "children" is used many times. John emphasizes the fact of the fellowship in the family. It is not only fellowship one with another but also with God the Father and with His Son, Jesus Christ.

In John's Gospel he tells us how we become children of God. "But as many as received him, to them gave he power to become the sons of God, even to them that believe on his name" (John 1:12). Here, in the Epistle, he shows us the blessings and responsibilities we have as the children of God.

The main theme of the Epistle is fellowship with God. In John's Gospel we have *life* through the Incarnate Word of God. In his Epistle, we have *fellowship* through the Incarnate Word of God.

The great yearning of the heart of God is that we should have fellowship with Him. The purpose of redemption is not just to free us from sin nor simply to get us to heaven, but rather to fit us for eternal, unbroken, wonderful, personal, intimate fellowship with the living God Himself. This is beyond all human comprehension. To accomplish this, He sent His Son into the human family for the purpose of redeeming out of the human family those men and women with whom He can have fellowship.

Sometimes people ask, "What about angels who have not sinned; why does God not have fellowship with them?" This I do not know, but one thing I do know! When a person receives the Saviour, he is brought into an intimate relationship with God Himself. It may be that only those who are redeemed from sin by Jesus Christ can appreciate the grace of God, the compassion, the tenderness, the love of God. It is blessedly true that those who love Him may have this wonderful fellowship with Him.

Thank God, we can enjoy this fellowship now. Some people are waiting for fellowship, with its joy and peace, until they get to heaven. My friend, God wants us to have it now. May I say that it is not that we are waiting to have fellowship with God, but God is waiting for us to have fellowship with Him!

You may say, "I am so frail, so weak, and I fail God so much." That may be true. As we well know, sin and disobedience break our fellowship. We find this true even in human relationships, and it is certainly also true with the divine relationship. However, John is dealing with the fact that even though we may fail God, He has made provision for forgiveness and cleansing, and He gives to us the ground for that cleansing. It would be well for us to remember that John gives us a declaration of Christ's accomplished work for us in the *past,* that is, His loving work of redemption (I John 4:9,10). He also informs us what Christ will do for us in the *future.* We shall be conformed to His image (I John 3:2). He reveals to us what Christ is doing for us *now.* Today, in heaven, He is praying for us. "If any man sin, we have an advocate with the Father, Jesus Christ the righteous" (I John 2:1).

THE PURPOSE OF THE FIRST EPISTLE OF JOHN

The purpose of the Epistle is threefold:

1. That your joy may be full.

> **And these things write we unto you, that your joy may be full (I John 1:4)**

Remember, our Lord has spoken so that His joy might remain in us and that our joy might be full (John 15:11). It is not God's desire that we go around with a long face or with a holier-than-thou expression. God wants us to have full joy. Full joy is found in Christ and is dependent upon full fellowship with Christ, the Incarnate Word of God.

Most of our joys down here are tarnished because of weakness, failure, misunderstandings, and sorrows of life. The world can have happiness which depends upon circumstances, but the world knows nothing of real joy. Our joy depends upon our relationship and fellowship with God. Even in the midst of sorrow and affliction we can have real, real joy. This is a wonderful thing! John writes these things unto us that our joy may be full.

2. That you sin not.

> **My little children, these things write I unto you, that ye sin not. And if any man sin, we have an advocate with the Father, Jesus Christ the righteous (I John 2:1).**

Sinning is inconsistent in one who is in fellowship with God. John writes to us that we might be free from sinning. He does not say that we have no sin. In fact, he says in the first chapter that if we say we have no sin, we deceive ourselves; we make Him a liar (I John 1:8.10). Because we do sin, provision has been made for us when we sin: "I write unto you, little children, because your sins are forgiven you for his name's sake" (I John 2:12). He has made it possible for us to be free from sin by forgiveness and cleansing through the work of Christ. Yet, John's great desire for us is that we should not sin. God Himself empowers us by the Spirit of God so that we may live lives glorifying to Him.

3. *That you may know that you have eternal life.*

These things have I written unto you that believe on the name of the Son of God; that ye may know that ye have eternal life (I John 5:13).

In the Gospel of John, eternal life is *granted* by believing the declaration of God, and His Word is always sure. The believer may not feel it; the believer may not know much about it. God has said it, and He always speaks the truth. "He that believeth on the Son hath everlasting life" (John 3:36).

In the Epistle of John, the believer *knows* that he has eternal life because he experiences Christ day by day in his life through fellowship. Thus, we can say with John, "Truly our fellowship is with the Father, and with his Son Jesus Christ" (I John 1:3).

Remember, the theme of the Epistle is *fellowship with God*. Wouldn't it be wonderful to read through the whole Epistle today, and keep this theme in mind while you read!

OUTLINE OF THE FIRST EPISTLE OF JOHN

I.   **The introduction to the Epistle (I John 1:1-4)**

      Life manifested in the Incarnate Word
      Life experienced by the Apostles
      Testimony given by the Apostles
      The Apostles' desire for us
      The result of fellowship with God

II. **Fellowship with God Who is Light (I John 1:5–2:28)**

      The message (I John 1:5)
      The test of our profession (I John 1:6-8)
      The provision for the restoration of fellowship
      (I John 1:9,10)
      The ground for fellowship with God
      (I John 2:1,2)
      The evidence of fellowship with God
      (I John 2:3-11)
            Obedience to His Word (3-5)
            Submission to His will (6-8)
            Love for the brethren (9-11)
      The place of the fellowship is in the family
      (I John 2:12-28)
            Declaration to the fathers (13,14)
            Address to the young men (13,14-17)
            Instructions to the little children (13,18-28)

III. **Fellowship with God Who is Righteous**
    (I John 2:29 - 4:6)

      The fact of God's righteousness (I John 2:29)
      The encouragement for fellowship (I John 3:1-3)
      The opposition to the fellowship (I John 3:4-13)
      The evidence of the fellowship (I John 3:14-18)

III. **Fellowship with God Who is Righteous, cont.**
    The result of the fellowship (I John 3:19-24)
        Assurance in fellowship (19-21)
        Assurance in prayer (22,23)
        Assurance because of our union with Him
        ✓(24)
    The test of the fellowship (I John 4:1-6)

IV. **Fellowship with God Who is Love (I John 4:7—5:5)**
    Divine love manifested (I John 4:7-10)
    The assurance of our union with Him
    (I John 4:11-19)
    Love manifested in His children (I John 4:20 -
    5:5)

V. **Divine Certainties and Assurances (I John 5:6 - 5:20)**

    Certainty of God's testimony (I John 5:6-8)
    Certainty of eternal life (I John 5:9-13)
    Certainty in prayer (I John 5:18-20)
    Certainty in victory (I John 5:18-20)

VI. **The Conclusion (I John 5:21)**

INTRODUCTION TO THE FIRST EPISTLE OF JOHN

It is usually true that in the introduction to a book we find the key to that book. In the first four verses of this Epistle we find the key.

> That which was from the beginning, which we have heard, which we have seen with our eyes, which we have looked upon, and our hands have handled, of the Word of life;
>
> (For the life was manifested, and we have seen it, and bear witness, and shew unto you that eternal life, which was with the Father, and was manifested unto us;)
>
> That which we have seen and heard declare we unto you, that ye also may have fellowship with us: and truly our fellowship is with the Father, and with his Son Jesus Christ.
>
> And these things write we unto you, that your joy may be full (I John 1:1-4).

LIFE MANIFESTED IN THE INCARNATE WORD

"That which was from the beginning..." It is very interesting to notice that in John's Gospel we have this statement, "In the beginning was the Word, and the Word was with God, and the Word was God. The same was in the beginning with God" (John 1:1,2). In the third verse of that chapter we learn that all things were made by Him (Jesus Christ), and this leads us back to the first verse of the Bible. "In the beginning God created the heaven and the earth" (Gen. 1:1). In the first verse of this Epistle which we are studying, we read, "That which was from the beginning." What are these three beginnings?

The word "beginning" in John's Gospel has to do with eternity, that which cannot be measured by time. "In the beginning was the Word." The beginning of what? Back just as far as one can go, before creation, He was there! The Word did not come into being, but was with God and was God. The Gospel of John starts with the pre-incarnate person of Jesus Christ.

In point of time, John 1:3 takes us back to Genesis 1:1, when, in the beginning, God created the heaven and the earth. Here is that time of creation when the worlds were made. John 1:3 tells us that all things were made by Him, and without Him was not anything made that was made. Genesis starts with God as the Creator and John informs us that Jesus Christ is the Creator.

The Epistle of John starts with the Incarnate Word of God. "That which was from the beginning, which we have heard, which we have seen ... " This was the beginning of our Lord's life among men, as a Man in the midst of men. This is comparable to the fourteenth verse in the first chapter of the Gospel of John: "And the Word was made flesh, and dwelt among us, (and we beheld his glory, the glory as of the only begotten of the Father), full of grace and truth" (John 1:14). Therefore, both the Gospel and the Epistle of John give to us the revelation of the Incarnate Son of God.

In the Gospel of John, there can be no life, divine life, imparted to us apart from *relationship* with the Incarnate Son of God. In the Epistle of John, there can be no *fellowship* with God apart from the Incarnate Word of God.

LIFE EXPERIENCED BY THE APOSTLES

That which was from the beginning, which we have heard, which we have seen with our eyes, which we have looked upon, and our hands have handled, of the Word of life ... (I John 1:1).

In this verse we have the testimony of those who knew the Lord in person and who walked with Him when He was on earth. What an experience these men must have had! Have you ever stopped to think how wonderful it must have been? They lived with the Saviour. They accompanied Him for three and a half years. They traveled with Him, ate with Him, slept with Him. They listened to His gracious words. They heard His claims of deity and saw His miracles. What a blessed sight to see Him heal the sick, cleanse the lepers, open the eyes of the blind, rebuke the fever. They were with Him when He fed the hungry and when He stilled the storm. No wonder they cried out, "What manner of man is this, that even the wind and the sea obey him?" (Mark 4:41).

Consider, for example, the feeding of the five thousand. He took the little boy's lunch of five loaves and two fishes, and looking up to heaven, He blessed them, broke them, and gave them to the disciples. Then, as the disciples gave the food to the multitude, it was multiplied. When they had fed the multitude, each disciple had a basketful left (Matt. 14:15-21). My, what an experience was theirs! We could spend much time thinking of the wonderful, miraculous things that happened in those three and a half years. This is what John is talking about in this verse.

You absolutely could not fool these men. They knew! "That which was from the beginning, which we have heard, which we have seen with our eyes, which we have looked upon, and our hands have handled . . . " Whom did they see and hear? The Word of Life!

I want you to know that He can be as real to you as He was to His disciples. My friend, you may not know much about doctrine, but if you have received the Saviour, you can have a real experience with God, just as these men did. You can experience His presence. You can rejoice in His fellowship. You can revel in His strength and power and can have full joy in Him. You can know His tenderness, His love, His comfort.

I have often wondered how these men felt when they went with Jesus to the tomb of Lazarus. You will recall that when Jesus said, "Take away the stone," Martha objected, "Don't do it! Leave it there because he is already in corruption, for he has been dead four days." Jesus answered, "Said I not unto thee, that, if thou wouldest believe, thou shouldest see the glory of God?" When they had taken away the stone, He said, "Lazarus, come forth!" Then said Jesus, "Loose him and let him go" (John 11:38-44). Remember this when you come to times of sorrow, when friends or family are taken home to God. You, too, can know what it is to experience the very presence of the One who said, "Because I live, ye shall live also" (John 14:19). "I am the resurrection, and the life: he that believeth in me, though he were dead yet shall he live . . . " (John 11:25).

John knew Him as a Man among men. He knew Him as the risen Saviour. This is the one who had his head upon His bosom. He had heard, had seen, had touched the Word of Life. So, in this verse he is able to tell us what he really *knows.* We too can know! I am sure that as we consider together the truths of this wonderful Epistle, the Word of Life will become more real and more precious to us.

TESTIMONY GIVEN BY THE APOSTLES

(For the life was manifested, and we have seen it, and bear witness, and shew unto you that eternal life, which was with the Father, and was manifested unto us;) (I John 1:2).

The Apostles not only experienced His presence, but they could not keep still about it. Dear Peter could say to the Sanhedrin, "We cannot but speak the things which we have seen and heard" (Acts 4:20). Even though they were threatened, they could not help but tell everything they knew about the Saviour. They were told to be quiet about this Jesus and not to talk about Him being raised from the dead. Peter said unto them, "Whether it be right in the sight of God to hearken unto you more than unto God, judge ye. For we cannot but speak the things which we have seen and heard" (Acts 4:19,20).

This second verse of the Epistle tells us of their witness. They told their friends. They told everyone. These converted commercial fishermen were transformed into flaming evangels of the gospel. They rejoiced in the fact that their Saviour lived; that the One with whom they had walked on earth before the cross had been raised from the dead; that He is the eternal Son of God. These disciples had heard our Saviour's last words before He ascended to the Father, "But ye shall receive power, after that the Holy Ghost is come upon you: and ye shall be witnesses unto me both in Jerusalem, and in all Judaea, and in Samaria, and unto the uttermost part of the earth" (Acts 1:8). "All power is given unto me in heaven and in earth. Go ye therefore, and teach all nations, baptizing them in the name of the Father, and of the Son, and of the Holy Ghost: Teaching them to observe all things whatsoever I have commanded you" (Matt. 28:18,19,20).

My friend, all over the world today there are hundreds upon hundreds of God's servants, living in shacks and grass huts, in the filth and dirt of some of those countries. Yet they have gone gladly, willing to sacrifice everything. What for? Because they love the Saviour and have experienced the blessedness of life in Him and cannot help but tell what they have seen and heard and know.

Perhaps you have belonged to a church all your life and you know all the doctrine of your church, but have not really experienced this life in Christ. Is this true of you? Or has the truth of the Word of God become a reality in your own heart and in your own life? When John uses "we," he is speaking for all the Apostles who said, "We have heard . . . we have seen . . . and bear witness, and shew unto you that eternal life, which was with the Father, and was manifested unto us." Can you say the same thing?

Do you remember the blind man in John 9? When the Pharisees spoke of Jesus, they said, "We know that this man is a sinner" (John 9:24). The blind man replied, "Whether he be a sinner or no, I know not: one thing I know, that, whereas I was blind, now I see" (John 9:25).

I can say to you today, my friend, as a personal testimony, that once I was blind but now I see. Once I was lost and now am found. Once I was afar off and now have been made nigh. Once I was a child of wrath, and now I am a child of God. I can say with Paul, "I know whom I have believed, and am persuaded that he is able to keep that which I have committed unto him against that day" (II Tim. 1:12). One day I shall stand in His presence, conformed to the image of His Son (Rom. 8:29). You cannot gainsay this! Not only does God's Word declare it, but my experience confirms it to my heart. His life has been manifested *to* me and *in* me. I know Him and I want to tell you about Him. I want you to know Him, too.

Friend, do you know Jesus Christ as your Saviour? Are these things real to you? Or is it just simply doctrine—cold, cold doctrine? This can become a living reality in your life if you mean business with God. God means business with you. Why did Jesus Christ become manifest in the flesh? So that *you* might have life: real life, eternal life, satisfying life, resurrection life! Where can this life be found? It can be found in Jesus Christ, God's Son, the Incarnate Word of God. I plead with your heart today, using the words of our Saviour when He said, "Come unto me, all ye that labour and are heavy laden, and I will give you rest" (Matt. 11:28). Again, "Him that cometh to me I will in no wise cast out" (John 6:37).

It makes no difference what your past experience has been, or how bad, how weak, how troubled you are now. His heart and His arms are always open to receive you. Why don't you come? This is a personal matter between you and Him. May you have that joy today!

THE APOSTLES' DESIRE FOR US

That which we have seen and heard declare we unto you, that ye also may have fellowship with us: and truly our fellowship is with the Father, and with his Son Jesus Christ (I John 1:3).

"That which we have seen and heard!" Notice, this is the third time he has mentioned it! "That which we have seen and heard we declare unto you." What for? "That ye also may have fellowship with us: and truly our fellowship is with the Father, and with his Son Jesus Christ." We are telling you that which we have seen and heard so that you might have the same intimacy with God that we have.

My Christian friend, you who have put your trust in the Saviour, do you know that the great yearning of God's heart is for your fellowship? How much of it do you give Him? How much of your time do you give to God? Sunday morning? Sunday school, maybe? Do you actually get into the Word of God and learn what He has to say to you? Do you have fellowship with Him in His Word? This is what John is talking about in this third verse.

Having spoken of his experience in verse one, and of his testimony in verse two, he now comes to his desire in verse three. John says that he is ministering the truth to us in order to bring us not only into relationship with the living God, (stated so clearly in John's Gospel), but also into intimate fellowship with Him.

Now, I want to stop here a moment, because it is difficult for me to put into words how I feel about this verse. John is saying to us, "We are preaching and teaching, ministering and sacrificing, so that you might clearly understand and enter into this same fellowship with us." John, what is this fellowship? It is true that we are brought into *relationship with God through faith in Christ,* but here, John is pleading that we may know in our *experience day by day, this fellowship with God.*

The enjoyment of spiritual life can come only as we walk in fellowship with God. A Spirit-filled life is the enjoyment of divine life; it is that life of fellowship. There is no higher experience for a believer, either on earth or in heaven, than the experience of personal, intimate fellowship with the living, sovereign, eternal God. The most amazing thing is that the grace of God has made this provision. His grace has redeemed us. But what is the purpose of all this redemption? God is going to have a people who will appreciate His love, His grace, His kindness, His very heart, and with whom He can have fellowship.

There are examples of this in the Old Testament. "And the LORD spake unto Moses face to face, as a man speaketh unto his friend" (Ex. 33:11). "And there arose not a prophet since in Israel like unto Moses, whom the LORD knew face to face" (Deut. 34:10). This is the great desire of God's heart! God had asked David to seek His face. "When thou saidst, Seek ye my face; my heart said unto thee, Thy face, LORD, will I seek" (Psa. 27:8). Notice that the request comes first from God. "David, I want your fellowship." David answers, "That's just what I want, Lord; I want Your fellowship."

This word "fellowship" carries with it the thought of partnership. It is like building a home with your beloved. You come to live together in that home and your life is one of loving partnership. Fellowship with God is being a partner with Him in His life, in His purpose, in His love, in all He is.

Let me illustrate what I mean. Paul asks, "Do ye not know that the saints shall judge the world? Know ye not that we shall judge angels? Know ye not that your body is the temple of the Holy Ghost which is in you?" (I Cor. 6:2,3,19). He says, "We are labourers together with God" (I Cor. 3:9). If we know these things, then how should we live among men? We are partakers with God, not only in His life, but in His purpose and in His will. This is to say, we are partners with God in His program of all that He is doing on earth and all that He is going to do in eternity. We are on "God's team" and therefore we must walk in a union with God. We must walk in fellowship with Him.

So then, what is God's purpose for men? It is that men might be redeemed. God is building a church, and He has called us to have a place as partners with Him in the building of His church. This is what John is talking about. Allow me to paraphrase, "That which we have heard, that which we have seen, we are declaring unto you that you might have partnership with us. Our partnership is with the Father and with His Son, Jesus Christ." My, what a calling! Partners with God! No wonder Paul could say that we are to walk according to our high calling in Christ Jesus (Eph. 4:1).

Jesus said, "I am in my Father, and ye in me, and I in you" (John 14:20).

"He that hath the Son hath life" (I John 5:12).

"We may have boldness in the day of judgment because as Christ is, so are we in this world" (I John 4:17).

We are not going to wait until we get to heaven to have eternal life, or to have a relationship with God, or to have fellowship with God. We *have* this relationship, this union with God, right now, and we *experience* this life by entering into fellowship with God. No wonder the next verse goes on to speak of our joy!

THE RESULT OF FELLOWSHIP WITH GOD

And these things write we unto you, that your joy may be full (I John 1:4).

The *source* of our joy is in God Himself, because of our relationship with Him. It thrills our hearts to know that we are the children of One who is God. The *nature* of our joy is having fellowship with Him. The *extent* of our joy is that it should be full. Full joy is God's desire for every one of His children.

"These things have I spoken unto you, that my joy might remain in you, and that your joy might be full" (John 15:11).

"Ask, and ye shall receive, that your joy may be full" (John 16:24).

"And now come I to thee; and these things I speak in the world, that they might have my joy fulfilled in themselves" (John 17:13).

The witness of John the Baptist concerning Jesus was, "This my joy therefore is fulfilled" (John 3:29).

Christian friend, are you experiencing full joy? Perhaps you say, "No, I'm in sorrow. I'm troubled and distressed and disturbed because of my own frailty." One man told me that he had more joy before he was a Christian than after he became a Christian. No, friend, there is no real joy before one becomes a Christian. That is happiness. One may have been happy because of circumstances. When the circumstances were good, there was happiness; when the circumstances were bad, there was unhappiness. I am not talking about that kind of up and down experience. I am talking about a joy that is God-given.

"These things have I spoken unto you, that my joy might remain in you" (John 15:11).

"Peace I leave with you, my peace I give unto you: not as the world giveth, give I unto you" (John 14:27).

"Because I live, ye shall live also" (John 14:19).

"But of Him are ye in Christ Jesus, who of God is made unto us wisdom and righteousness and sanctification, and redemption" (I Cor. 1:30). Jesus is my joy, my peace, my life, my righteousness. Circumstances do not affect this God-given joy!

This does not mean that we are always going to be hilarious, or be putting on a false front, or be trying to make believe that we are happy. Instead, there comes a settledness, a quiet satisfaction, an assurance, a peace, a joy that is beyond the ken of men. The circumstances of life do not affect this joy or this peace. John is saying, "This is why I am writing to you, that your joy may be full."

FELLOWSHIP
WITH GOD
WHO IS LIGHT

> This then is the message which we have heard of Him, and declare unto you, that God is light, and in him is no darkness at all (I John 1:5).

We have come now to the first main division of the book. There are three statements concerning the nature of God in this Epistle:

God is light. That is, God is absolute in holiness.

God is righteous. That is, He is right in everything He does and every act of His is right.

God is love. That is, love characterizes the energy of His nature toward men.

The first of these statements is that God is light, and in Him is no trace of darkness. We read of our Saviour in I Timothy 6:16, "Who only hath immortality, dwelling in the light which no man can approach unto." This is God's absolute holiness in character.

God, being light, *must* reveal Himself. Remember that in Exodus 19 at the giving of the law the Lord said, "Lo, I come unto thee in a thick cloud" (Ex. 19:9). The people were full of fear and trembled. But now God has come out into the light! "The darkness is past, and the true light now shineth" (I John 2:8). *God has revealed Himself.* He has come out into the light in Christ Jesus, who has purged our sins, who has removed the barrier between God and man, who has rent the veil. "God who at sundry times and in divers manners spake in time past unto the fathers by the prophets, hath in these last days spoken unto us by his Son" (Heb. 1:1,2).

However, we find that when He came, men refused the light. In the Gospel of John we read, "In him was life; and the life was the light of men. And the light shineth in darkness; and the darkness comprehended it not. There was a man sent from God, whose name was John. The same came for a witness, to bear witness of the Light, that all men through him might believe. He was not that Light, but was sent to bear witness of that Light. That was the true Light, which lighteth every man that cometh into the world" (John 1:4-9).

Do you mean to tell me that men were in such moral darkness, such spiritual darkness, that God had to send someone to bear witness of the Light? That is true. They would not hear the witness, nor would they turn to the One who is the true Light, so they remained in darkness.

The purpose of light is to dispel darkness. When light shines, the darkness is gone. Men were in darkness concerning God, but He came into the world to "shine in our hearts, to give the light of the knowledge of the glory of God in the face of Jesus Christ" (II Cor. 4:6). He came that we might know Him; that we might know truly who He is and what we are; that we might know His person, the One who is "full of grace and truth" (John 1:14); that we might know His purpose in redeeming us, in giving us the gift of eternal life, and bringing us into relationship and fellowship with Himself; that He might bring us "out of darkness into his marvellous light" (I Peter 2:9). We are not now in darkness, but we are in Him in whom is no darkness at all. "For ye were sometimes darkness, but now are ye light in the Lord: walk as children of light" (Eph. 5:8).

THE TEST OF OUR PROFESSION

If we claim to be in fellowship with God, certainly we must be willing to be tested. If we come to believe certain truths and consider ourselves to be a certain type of person, then we will prove it by the way we live and walk. So we read:

If we say that we have fellowship with him, and walk in darkness, we lie, and do not the truth:

But if we walk in the light, as he is in the light, we have fellowship one with another, and the blood of Jesus Christ his Son cleanseth us from all sin.

If we say that we have no sin, we deceive ourselves, and the truth is not in us (I John 1:6-8).

Many people say that they can understand how we can have fellowship with a God who is love but cannot understand how we can have fellowship with a God who is absolute in holiness, with One who is absolutely righteous in His character and in His acts, with One who is light and in whom is no darkness at all. Listen, friend, the most amazing truth of all time is that our Saviour left the glory and came to earth for the purpose of preparing a people with whom He could have fellowship. The barrier between God and man has been removed and *God is accessible.* "Having, therefore, brethren, boldness to enter into the holiest by the blood of Jesus, by a new and living way, which he hath consecrated for us, through the veil, that is to say, his flesh; And having an high priest over the house of God; Let us draw near with a true heart in full assurance of faith" (Heb. 10:19-22). This is a wonderful fact. But we need to ask ourselves some questions. Do I draw near? Do I walk in fellowship with Him?

The following verses present to us the test of our profession. Notice:

"if we say" in verse six,
"if we walk" in verse seven,
"if we say" in verse eight,
"if we confess" in verse nine,
"if we say" in verse ten,
"he that saith" in chapter two, verses four, six, and nine.
Christianity is more than doctrine; it is more than just
talking about truth. A Christian is one in whom truth lives.
There can be no real life at all until we are in right
relationship with the Saviour. And the truth does not live
in us unless we are in fellowship with Him. If we are in
fellowship with Him, and if we make a profession of such
fellowship, then we will be tested. "If we say that we have
fellowship with him, and walk in darkness, we lie, and do
not the truth" (I John 1:6).

John puts it into very simple language. If we claim to
belong to the kingdom of light and claim to have fellowship with God, but are walking in darkness, then we
certainly are not telling the truth. It is impossible to walk
in darkness when we are in right relationship with the One
who is light. This would be an absolute inconsistency. Also,
we will notice, as we read the Epistle, that John talks
about light and darkness and there is no grey zone
between. We are either in light or we are in darkness. We
are either in the kingdom of light or in the kingdom of
darkness. We are either children of God or we are the
children of the devil.

Do you remember that amazing passage written by Paul
in Colossians? "Giving thanks unto the Father, which hath
made us meet to be partakers of the inheritance of the
saints in light: Who hath delivered us from the power of
darkness, and hath translated us into the kingdom of his
dear Son" (Col. 1:12,13).

This translation into a new kingdom occurred the moment you and I accepted the Saviour. Every real Christian
is in the kingdom of light, has been removed from the
kingdom of darkness, and has been translated into the

kingdom of His dear Son. We are no longer in the dark. God no longer sees us in the kingdom of darkness. If we have received Jesus Christ as our Saviour, God declares us to be in *His* kingdom. But if we say that we are in fellowship with God who is light, and are living in darkness, we are not telling the truth. We cannot for one moment live in the kingdom of darkness after He has translated us into the kingdom of light.

I think Paul had this same thought in mind in his writing: "God forbid that I should glory, save in the cross of our Lord Jesus Christ, by whom the world is crucified unto me, and I unto the world" (Gal. 6:14). Whether one is a Jew or Gentile does not make any difference "for in Christ Jesus neither circumcision availeth any thing, nor uncircumcision, but a new creature" (Gal. 6:15). We are a new creation! Paul restates this in the letter to Corinth where he is speaking of the risen, glorified Christ and of any man who is in this Christ, this risen Christ. "Though we have known Christ after the flesh, yet now henceforth know we him no more. Therefore if any man be in Christ, he is a new creature: old things are passed away; behold, all things are become new" (II Cor. 5:16,17).

This is the position into which God has placed *His* people. This does not mean that we will not fail God. We will discuss that in a moment. Even in our failure, we are still in the kingdom of light. *This is where we live.*

John clearly states that a person is either in the light or in the dark. If we say that we are living in the kingdom of light, in God's kingdom, in fellowship with God, and we walk in darkness and live like those who are in the dark, then we are liars. He states the same truth in the second chapter. He is speaking about the unsaved person when he writes, "He that saith he is in the light, and hateth his brother, is in darkness even until now . . . But he that hateth his brother is in darkness, and walketh in darkness, and knoweth not whither he goeth, because that darkness hath blinded his eyes." (I John 2:9,11).

Is it not wonderful to know that when you trusted the Saviour, God took you out of the kingdom of darkness and put you into the kingdom of God's dear Son? We are no longer seen in sin but in Christ. We are no longer in darkness, but in light. We are no longer under judgment, but are righteous in Christ.

However, we must face the fact that Christians do fail God. Christians do sin. In fact, verse eight tells us that "if we say we have no sin, we deceive ourselves, and the truth is not in us." Let us never fool ourselves. People who boast about not sinning are actually proud of what they are or think they are. And what is pride but the root sin? We do fail God, every one of us.

This passage is not talking about *how* we walk but *where* we walk. If we walk in the light, as He is in the light, and if we fail God, then the blood of Jesus Christ His Son cleanses us from all sin. *He keeps on keeping us clean.* Remember, this is talking about those who are walking in the light, not those who are in the kingdom of darkness. This is talking about God's people. Where do we walk? We walk in the light. Do we always walk in fellowship with the One who is light? I am sorry to say, "No!" But when we do fail, we are restored, because the blood of Christ cleanses us from all sin.

There is a difference between *relationship* to Christ and *fellowship* with Him. Here John is not talking about relationship with God. That has been forever settled. There is only one place where a Christian can walk and that is in the light, in the kingdom of God. Here he is talking about fellowship with God who is light. The Christian who fails God breaks fellowship with God. This does not take him out of the kingdom of God. It does not change his position before God. *He is still a member of God's family.*

God, who is absolute in holiness, has prepared a people who are able to come into His presence. It is a marvelous, wonderful, glorious thing that God has taken men and women who had rebelled against Him, who had been ungodly, who had been sinners, and has forgiven them, justified them, translated them out of the kingdom of darkness into the kingdom of His dear Son forever. In this kingdom of His Son we who have been redeemed do still fail God because our bodies are not yet glorified. However, our lives are no longer characterized by sin.

"If we say that we have no sin, we deceive ourselves." Indeed, we do not deceive anybody else, certainly not those who live around us. Some people say, "I do not sin, I only make mistakes." Well, my friend, let us label sin as sin. Let us not try to rationalize it away. That which is out of the will of God, which does not conform to the very character of God, is sin. I John 3:4 tells us that sin is lawlessness.

Let us remember that the cleansing is for those who are walking in the light. Did you ever stop to think that those who are told to confess their sin are those who are in the kingdom of light, who are in touch with the Saviour? The man who is not in Christ Jesus, who is in the world, who walks in the kingdom of darkness, is the man who does not care whether or not he is in sin. When one points out to such a person that he is a sinner, his answer is likely to be, "I'm just as good as you are!" Of course, that may be true. But is that what he is going to tell God? Can he stand in the presence of God with such a poor excuse? The man out of Christ does not think about his sin with great concern. The really concerned man is the one who has come to the Saviour. The more one knows the Saviour, the more one realizes his own weakness and failure. Permit me to give some examples of this from the Scriptures.

Job is the oldest book in the Bible and is possibly the oldest book ever written. Job lived around 1500 to 2000 B.C. In the first two chapters of that book God is talking with Satan concerning Job. He said to Satan, "Have you seen my servant Job? He is a good man. He loves the good and hates the evil. You cannot find a flaw in Job." Then God began to deal with Job. Job was good, but he was also self-righteous. When he walked down the streets, the young men would bow before him. When he sat in the gates of the city, everyone had respect for him. They listened to his counsel. Yet God permitted Job to go through a terrible time of testing. He was smitten with a loathsome disease. His philosophical friends came and sat down with him and spent seven days just sitting and weeping because of the awful condition of Job. Through many of the chapters of Job these friends tried to reason with him about his condition. Then Elihu, the servant of God, came and he could not get anywhere with Job. Finally God came on the scene and met Job. Do you know what Job said when he had seen the Lord? "I have heard of thee by the hearing of the ear: but now mine eye seeth thee. Wherefore I abhor myself, and repent in dust and ashes" (Job 42:5,6).

You do not find an unsaved man saying that! This is a good man. What made him say it? *He had had a glimpse of Christ.* The trouble today is that people have never seen Christ in all His beauty and righteousness. Most people have dethroned Christ. They make Him a teacher, or a good man, or a moralist with wonderful, ethical instructions. They will not give Him His rightful place as the Son of God, God manifest in the flesh. The result is that they have no conviction of sin.

Consider Isaiah who was possibly one of the most astounding men of his day. This man prophesied during the reign of four kings. He went into the presence of the kings of Israel and felt perfectly at ease. He was one of the greatest prophets in the Old Testament, the prophet of redemption. Yet, listen to him in chapter six; "In the year that king Uzziah died I saw also the Lord sitting upon a throne, high and lifted up, and his train filled the temple. Above it stood the seraphims: ... And one cried unto another, and said, Holy, holy, holy, is the LORD of hosts: the whole earth is full of his glory" (Isa. 6:1-3). What a wonderful picture. And then this man cried out, "Woe is me! for I am undone; because I am a man of unclean lips, and I dwell in the midst of a people of unclean lips: for mine eyes have seen the King, the LORD of hosts" (Isa. 6:5). What opened Isaiah's eyes to his condition? *Seeing the Lord.* What people know more about sin and the awfulness of sin than those who walk in the light? The very light of God shines into the darkness of men's hearts and consciences.

There is nothing in the whole book of Daniel that is derogatory about Daniel, the prophet. In fact, he is called a comely person. Yet, after he saw the Lord, he said, "My comeliness was turned in me into corruption" (Daniel 10:8).

Consider Peter in Luke, chapter five. The Lord was preaching to the crowd from the boat and He said to Peter, "Launch out into the deep, and let down your nets for a draught." Peter answered, "Master, we have toiled all the night, and have taken nothing; nevertheless at thy word I will let down the net." In obedience to Christ they caught a harvest of fish. Then what did Peter do? He fell down at the knee of Jesus and said, "Depart from me; for I am a sinful man, O Lord" (Luke 5:1-11). What moved Peter to say that? *He had seen the revelation of the Son of God.*

What I am trying to get to your heart is this: when we have seen the Lord, when we really know Him, then we recognize our own sinfulness and our own inability to do the things we should do. We realize the need to walk continually in fellowship with Him. When we do walk in the light and are in fellowship with the One who is light, then we will have fellowship one with another. And the blood of Jesus Christ will cleanse from all sin. Why should we need cleansing if we are sinless and without weakness and failure? Again I come back to it. When we accepted the Saviour, we were transformed into the children of God and took our place in the kingdom of light. This is where we are. This is where we live. This is where we walk. But there are times when we fail God. *This breaks our fellowship with God who is light — not the relationship but the fellowship.* When this happens, we can know that He has made provision for us. We rejoice in the fact that the blood of Jesus Christ keeps on keeping us clean. When our fellowship with Him is broken, He will restore and cleanse us.

May you live in wonderful fellowship with Him today!

THE PROVISION FOR THE
RESTORATION OF FELLOWSHIP

If we confess our sins, he is faithful and just to forgive us our sins, and to cleanse us from all unrighteousness.

If we say that we have not sinned, we make him a liar, and his word is not in us (I John 1:9,10).

When the Lord Jesus died to put away our sins, He did a perfect work. He made it possible for us to come into right relationship with God, to become His children, to be pardoned every sin, and to be fitted for His presence. This relationship cannot be broken. Even though we fail and are weak and stumbling, we are still the objects of His love. "Having loved his own which were in the world, he loved them unto the end" (John 13:1).

The great yearning of God's heart is that His people, His children, might have real fellowship with Him. I love to watch school children run home to Mother and see her take them in her arms and hug them. I have wondered, how do we, the children of God, treat the living God who redeemed us? We boast about being His children, but how much fellowship do we have with Him? How much do we seek to please His heart? Paul's hope was that Christ should be "magnified in my body, whether it be by life, or by death" (Phil. 1:20).

In verse eight it was stated that the reality of sinfulness may be denied by some. "If we say that we have no sin . . . " There are those who say there is no principle of sin in a person and that sin is just an hallucination of the mind. When we read verse nine, however, we must admit the reality of sin along with Isaiah and Job and Daniel and Peter. We admit that Christians do sin. We also accept the divine provision for restoration to fellowship.

Walking in the light brings a consciousness of guilt which breaks the fellowship. We cannot divorce verse seven from verse nine. In verse seven the very walking in the light of God's Word, or in the light of His Person, reveals what we are. We acknowledge the fact that we do sin and that God is righteous. Then in verse nine, "If we confess our sins, he is faithful and just to forgive us our sins, and to cleanse us from all unrighteousness." It is not "faithful and merciful" nor even "faithful and loving" but "faithful and *just (righteous)* to forgive us our sins and to cleanse us from all unrighteousness." Let me assure you of one thing. God will keep His Word! When we confess our sins, we are *forgiven and cleansed.*

This is different from the way we entered into *relationship* with God. At the cross we received forgiveness. The moment we became Christians we were forgiven every sin. *He did not ask us to confess our sin. He asked us to receive the Saviour.* The moment we took Jesus Christ as our Saviour, on the ground of His wonderful grace, He forgave our sin.

"In whom we have redemption through his blood, the forgiveness of sins, ACCORDING TO THE RICHES OF HIS GRACE" (Eph. 1:7).

"And be ye kind one to another, tenderhearted, forgiving one another, even as God FOR CHRIST'S SAKE hath forgiven you" (Eph. 4:32).

"I write unto you, little children, because your sins are forgiven you FOR HIS NAME'S SAKE" (I John 2:12).

We are forgiven according to the riches of His grace, for Christ's sake, for His name's sake. This is true for all God's people!

However, *restoration to fellowship is dependent upon confession.* There are Christians who say that it is all right to sin over and over, and go on sinning, because all they need to do is confess. Let us not fool ourselves. That is not true confession. Honest confession includes a sorrow for what we have done and a desire to do what is right. If we feel that we can continue to sin because we can confess and be forgiven, we have no conception of the heart and character of God. We have no understanding of the absolute righteousness and holiness of the One with whom we have fellowship. Our fellowship is with God who is light!

Listen, my friend, if you say that you can confess your sin, be forgiven, and go right on sinning, then not only do you fail to understand the holiness of God, but you do not have an appreciation of what He has done for you, nor do you understand your position in Him. You can be sure that if you are a child of God, you will be disciplined by Him. "For whom the Lord loveth he chasteneth" (Heb. 12:6). Why? That we might yield "the peaceable fruit of right-eousness" (Heb. 12:11).

Please, be honest and real in your confession. When you confess your sin, name the thing which has broken the fellowship. Don't get down beside your bed at night and say, "Dear Lord, forgive me for my sins today." This is not true confession. When we confess, we should tell the Lord the thing that we have done and ask His forgiveness and cleansing. When we have sinned against someone else, we should also go to them. *Keep short accounts with God.* Do not wait until Sunday morning to confess a sin. Do not wait until the awareness of wrong-doing wears off. Even Abraham, the friend of God, reaped the fruitage of un-judged sin in his life. We cannot get away from the fact that God must judge sin.

We may say, "But I am a child of God." Well and good! A child of God may be out of fellowship with God, for *sin breaks fellowship.* How often, then, should we confess? As often as we sin. When we confess, we are forgiven and cleansed.

Is it not true that oftentimes, after we confess our sin, we go on about our work and we are still thinking about the sin which we have committed? I have experienced this and probably you have, too. The result is that it is the sin which is on our mind. Soon we find ourselves doing the same thing again. Why not believe what He has said? "If we confess our sins, he is faithful and just to forgive us our sins, and TO CLEANSE US from all unrighteousness." The moment we do this, our fellowship is restored. Then let us really believe this and turn our thought from ourselves and our sin to Jesus Christ, the Saviour.

It is possible for a believer to live every day in fellowship with Christ. We may fail God, but we come to the Lord, sometimes with a broken heart. We don't even know why we did what we did. A man came to me for counselling, and he had done something that really shocked me. I asked, "Why in the world did you do it?" He answered, "Mr. Mitchell, I don't know why I did it. I am so ashamed and sorry. I want to be forgiven and cleansed." I tell you, it is a wonderful thing to go with a man in that condition, one who really means business with God, to the throne of grace to be cleansed. God has made known to us the wonderful provision for fellowship with Him and *when we meet the condition, He will keep His promise.* "If we confess our sins, he is faithful and just to forgive us our sins, and to cleanse us from all unrighteousness."

When you realize that something has come between you and your Lord, do not go another hour out of fellowship with Him. *You are not waiting for God. God is waiting for you.* Confess your sin and be cleansed. He knows all about it. He is your Father. Then enjoy the day in fellowship with Him. It will delight the heart of God, and it will fill you with great joy.

Let us turn to the Old Testament for a wonderful illustration of the truth of God's provision for the restoration of fellowship. After Israel had come out of Egypt, they suffered thirst, and they cried unto Moses and Aaron, who, in turn, cried unto God. God said, "Behold, I will stand before thee there upon the rock in Horeb; and thou shalt smite the rock, and there shall come water out of it, that the people may drink." Moses took the rod of God and smote the rock, and water came forth, life-giving water, for the people who were thirsty. Nothing is said about the condition of the people except that they were thirsty, and God met their need in a very remarkable way (Exodus 17:1-7).

In the Book of Numbers, chapter 20, they were thirsty again, and they were ready to kill Moses, so Moses came before the Lord. "And the LORD spake unto Moses, saying, Take the rod, and gather thou the assembly together, thou, and Aaron thy brother, and speak ye unto the rock before their eyes; and it shall give forth his water, and thou shalt bring forth to them water out of the rock." Now, mark the change. You *speak* to the rock. You remember how Moses came to the people and said, "Hear now, ye rebels; must WE fetch you water out of this rock?" And he smote the rock twice. The water came out, but Moses came under the judgment of God (Num. 20:2-13). Why did he? What had he done wrong? Let us turn to the New Testament to see.

I Corinthians 10 reiterates the history of Israel, and Paul writes that "they drank of that spiritual Rock that followed them: and that Rock was Christ" (I Cor. 10:4). In other words, the rock in Exodus 17 is a type of Christ, who was smitten for us. Because Christ was smitten for us, we receive that life-giving water. That is, when we come to the One who died for us and rose again, and when we accept Him as our Saviour, then we are cleansed and forgiven every sin. We receive life eternal.

But now, even as Christians, we sin. What shall we do? Go back to the cross and be saved over again? No! Christ died for our sins only once. We need to *speak* to the Rock.

God had told Moses to speak to the rock and it would give forth its water. We are to confess our sins. *We go to the throne. We do not go back to the cross.*

In the Book of Hebrews we are encouraged, "Let us therefore come boldly unto the throne of grace, that we may obtain mercy, and find grace to help in time of need" (Heb. 4:16). Come with boldness! To whom is this written? To those Christians who are in need of mercy. Who needs mercy? The Christians who fail. To these He says, "Come, do not be afraid. Confess your sins. Speak to the Rock."

The Rock was smitten for us *once.* Christ will never again go to the cross. He gave His life *once* for all, forever. He perfectly completed the task He came to do. Notice how the following verses emphasize this.

"But now ONCE in the end of the world hath he appeared to put away sin by the sacrifice of himself" (Heb. 9:26). ("World" in this verse is literally "age.")

"But this man, after he had offered ONE sacrifice for sins for ever, sat down on the right hand of God" (Heb. 10:12).

"For in that he died, he died unto sin ONCE: but in that he liveth, he liveth unto God" (Rom. 6:10).

I would like to speak of this from a different viewpoint. *Riches of grace* are ours because of Christ's sacrifice for us. We are saved according to the riches of His grace. "For by grace are ye saved through faith" (Eph. 2:8). Riches of grace proceed from the cross. Now that we are believers, our daily needs are met according to His *riches in glory.* Paul prayed that we might be made powerfully strong according to His riches in glory (Eph. 3:16,17). Again, in Philippians 4:19, "But my God shall supply all your need according to his riches in glory by Christ Jesus." It is by the riches of grace that we are saved. It is by the riches of glory that our present needs are met. We do not go back to the cross to be saved over again. We do confess our sins to the One who is now on the throne, and He has promised to forgive and cleanse.

Let us consider one more example. In John 13 our Lord began to wash the disciples' feet and Peter said, "Lord, You shall never wash my feet." The Lord answered, "If I wash thee not, thou hast no part with Me." "Well, Lord, if it means that, why don't You just wash me completely?" The Lord's amazing answer was, "He that is washed needeth not save to wash his feet, but is clean every whit: and ye are clean, but not all. For he knew who should betray him; therefore said he, Ye are not all clean" (John 13:4-11). *At the cross we were bathed. His present ministry is to keep us clean now.*

If you have accepted the Saviour, and yet your life has been robbed of joy, of blessing, and of peace, you cannot go back to the cross. You have access to the throne of God. Speak to the One who is on the throne. Tell Him about your sin, your weakness, your frailty, your failure. He will forgive and cleanse and will fill your life with joy and peace as you walk in fellowship with Him.

Let us be occupied with Him! Let us live for His glory! Let us be ambitious to be found pleasing to God!

THE GROUND FOR FELLOWSHIP WITH GOD

> My little children, these things write I unto you, that ye sin not. And if any man sin, we have an advocate with the Father, Jesus Christ the righteous:
>
> And he is the propitiation for our sins: and not for ours only, but also for the sins of the whole world (I John 2:1,2).

A problem has been raised in the previous chapter. If we say we have fellowship with Him, and we walk in darkness, then we are lying (I John 1:6). If we say that we have no sin, then we are deceiving ourselves and not telling the truth (I John 1:8). If we say that we have not sinned, we make God a liar (I John 1:10). Since sin is universal, it would seem that it must be inevitable that we sin, and so we try to excuse ourselves. Even we who are Christians may say that we can't help it when we sin because everybody sins.

John certainly does not excuse sin. Sin is a terrible thing! It was sin that caused the Saviour to go to the cross to die for men. It was sin that took men away from God. It was sin that brought a barrier between God and man. Christ came to give His life for us that He might remove that barrier. It is now possible for us to come into the very presence of God through faith in our Lord Jesus Christ, who died to put away our sins. When we once understand the greatness of Christ's sacrifice for us, the fulness of His pardon, and the excellence of all that He has made possible for us, then we will see the awfulness of sin, and we will not want to continue in sin. "My little children, these things write I unto you, that ye sin not." Sinning is inconsistent in one who is walking in the light.

In this chapter John is pleading for *moral fitness,* for day by day walking with God. May I remind you that he is not dealing with *judicial fitness,* which was forever settled at the cross. Our *position* before God cannot be changed. He is dealing here with the matter of *fellowship* with God. Again I repeat it, because I want it clearly in your minds. We have bodies that have desires and lusts that are contrary to the character and will of God. Even though we yearn for the things of God, we do things that we should not do. Paul says, "What I would, that I do not; but what I hate, that I do" (Rom. 7:15). So we have a real problem with these bodies that are not yet glorified.

God has made the provision for our restoration into fellowship with Him, and this was stated in chapter one in verses nine and ten. If we confess, He forgives and cleanses. *The ground for this fellowship is the work of Christ.*

May I remind you that our Lord's work for us is threefold. He has finished one work at the cross and in resurrection when He put away sin by the sacrifice of Himself. He has made possible the redemption of men because He satisfied the very character of God and reconciled men to God. He has made it possible for God to declare righteous every sinner who believes in Jesus Christ. On the cross He said, "It is finished." *This work has been completed.*

In the *future,* our Lord will do another work. He will return to the earth to reign as King of kings and Lord of lords. He will first judge the nations and Israel. Then He will set up His glorious kingdom and reign for a thousand years on earth. All nations will be under his banner and the knowledge of the Lord shall cover the earth as the waters cover the sea. The nations shall learn war no more, and He will arbitrate between the nations (Isa. 11).

In the *present,* Jesus has a ministry at the right hand of God. The entire Book of Hebrews deals with our Saviour on the throne of grace as our *High Priest.* He is our Representative, our Intercessor, our Forerunner, our Refuge, our Hope—all that we need. This is stated in Hebrews where God is set forth in His governmental dealings with His people. In the Epistle of John, we learn that He prays for us in our frailty. This is another aspect of Christ's *present ministry:* the *advocacy of Christ* in making provision for His people when they sin. One of the results of His advocacy for us when we sin is that the fellowship in the family is restored. "If any man sin, we have an advocate with the Father, Jesus Christ the righteous."

Notice, it doesn't say that if any man repent, he has an Advocate; nor if any man promises to be good, he has an Advocate. If any man *sin,* he has an Advocate. He is not talking to the unsaved. The unsaved man needs the work of the cross. He needs a Saviour. This is speaking to the Christian who has received eternal life as a gift and now wants to walk in fellowship with God. The *believer who sins is the one who needs an Advocate.*

We do not read in Scripture that we have an Advocate with God, nor do we read that we have a High Priest with the Father. In the Book of Hebrews, God is set forth in His *governmental* dealing with His people, and Christ is revealed in His present ministry before God as our High Priest. We need a High Priest because we are here in frailty and weakness. In the Epistle of John, we are taught that the Father and those who believe in His Son are in a *family* relationship, and fellowship is a family matter. We have an Advocate with the *Father!* He effectively pleads our cause before the Father. He does this pleading on the ground that He has already, and still continues, to satisfy perfectly the demands of divine holiness. *He is the abiding propitiation.*

Now we come to the question: When does He start to plead our cause? When we sin? Before we sin? After we confess? When is He our Advocate? My friend, He is *always* our Advocate. He is continually pleading our cause. Let me illustrate this with our Lord's advocacy for Peter.

In Luke 22 the Lord said, "Simon, Simon, behold, Satan hath desired to have you, that he may sift you as wheat: But I have prayed for thee, that thy faith fail not" (Luke 22:31,32). Notice that Jesus did not pray that he would not sin or that he would not deny Him. He had already talked to the Father and had pleaded his cause so that his *faith* would not fail. Peter did not know himself, and he replied, "Lord, I am ready to go with thee, both into prison, and to death" (Luke 22:33). Peter is saying, "You can surely count on me. I know the rest of them here may fail you, but you can count on me. I'll die for You." And Peter meant every word of it.

When we think of Peter sinning, we think of him denying his Lord with oaths and curses. We must remember that it didn't start there. It started with *self-confidence.* Peter had confidence in the flesh.

In the Garden of Gethsemane our Lord had asked Peter, James, and John to watch with Him, but when He came back to them, He found Peter *sleeping* (Matt. 26:36-46). It is always easier to sleep than it is to pray. When the crowd came to take the Lord captive in the garden, Peter took out his sword and cut off a fellow's ear. The Lord had just demonstrated His power by declaring who He is, and they had all fallen backwards to the ground. That was a manifestation of the power of God. But then Peter took out his sword and manifested the *flesh* (John 18:1-11).

After the soldiers had taken Jesus, Peter *followed afar off.* In the palace of the high priest he *sat down with the enemies of Christ* and warmed himself at their fire. Then he *denied* his Lord three times (John 18:12-27; Luke 22:54-62).

If we note the steps in Peter's downfall, we find that he was boastful. He slept when he should have been praying. He acted in the energy of the flesh when he cut off the ear of Malchus. He followed afar off. He sat down with the enemies of Christ. He denied the Saviour, adding his oaths and curses.

Then the Lord turned and looked on Peter, and Peter went out and wept bitterly. He did not lose his love for the Saviour. He did not lose his faith in the Saviour. *Peter* failed miserably but his *faith* did not fail. Peter's faith did not fail because of the advocacy of Christ, our Lord. He had pleaded Peter's cause, that his *faith* fail not, and if you tell me that Peter lost his faith, then I must tell you that the prayers of Christ were not efficacious. They were not enough. No, you must confess with me that if Jesus Christ is God's Son, the righteous One, then His prayer must avail for His people. In fact, I am convinced that if it were not for His prayers for the people of God, not one could stand. Not for a moment! He effectively pleads our cause. He never tires of pleading our cause.

Do you realize that we have two Advocates? We have Jesus Christ in heaven as our Advocate, pleading our cause before the Father so that our fellowship might be restored and that we might be filled with joy and with blessing (I John 2:1,2). Also, the Spirit of God is an Advocate, dwelling in us, pleading His cause in us (Rom. 8:26,27).

How wonderful it is that God has supplied three deterrents to sin. *He has given us His Word.* "Thy word have I hid in mine heart, that I might not sin against thee" (Psa. 119:11). "Now ye are clean through the word which I have spoken unto you" (John 15:3). And, *He has given us His Holy Spirit,* indwelling us to lead and guide and direct us in our living (John 16:13). He longs to have us know and obey His Word and to have us submit to the leading of the Holy Spirit. *He has given us an Advocate, the Lord Jesus Christ.*

Notice that our Advocate with the Father is "Jesus Christ, the righteous." He is the sinless One. Here He is not called Jesus Christ, the merciful One, or the loving One, or the compassionate One, or the tender One. No! The issue here is sin, sin as opposed to righteousness. When you and I sin, we have a righteous God involved. How, then, can a righteous God forgive us our sin? Here is the answer. "We have an advocate with the Father, JESUS CHRIST THE RIGHTEOUS: and HE is the propitiation for our sins: and not for our's only, but also for the sins of the whole world."

Did you ever fall in love with Christ? If you love the Saviour, do you know that you stand before God in all the righteousness of Christ? God never sees us apart from His Son. He always see us clothed in the garments of *His* righteousness. What a peace that brings us! What a Saviour!

> **And he is the propitiation for our sins: and not for ours only, but also for the sins of the whole world (I John 2:2)**

The Greek word for "propitiation" is the same word used for "mercy-seat." It signifies that which Christ has become for the sinner. On the cross He met the demands of God's holiness and righteousness. He is what the mercy-seat was in the Old Testament, namely, the place of meeting between God and men. John is telling us in these verses that Christ is our Advocate, not only because He is the righteous One, but also because He is the abiding propitiation for our sin.

"Being justified freely by his grace through the redemption that is in Christ Jesus: Whom God hath set forth to be a propitiation through faith in his blood, to declare his righteousness for the remission of sins that are past, through the forbearance of God; To declare, I say, at this time his righteousness: that he might be just, and the justifier of him which believeth in Jesus" (Romans 3:24-26).

When Christ died on the cross, He vindicated the righteous character of God; He perfectly satisfied all the divine character. In other words, the eternal God in all His holiness and justice and righteousness was perfectly and completely satisfied with what Jesus Christ, His Son, accomplished on the cross. *This is God's side of Calvary.* Our side is to be redeemed and reconciled.

The important issue is that God is satisfied with the work of His Son. It is not our value of the blood of Christ that saves us and cleanses us. It is the great value that God has put upon the blood of His Son. *God is satisfied!* Christ is the propitiation for our sins. This is ever the basis of our Lord's advocacy. He pleads our cause on the ground that He has already satisfied the divine character of God for us.

"He is the propitiation for our sins: and not for our's only, but also for the sins of the whole world." There is sufficient value in the work of Christ, who satisfied the character of God, for the whole world to be saved if they would but come to Him. A complete work was accomplished at the cross. Divine righteousness was perfectly and fully satisfied once for all. This is the statement in Romans. Here, in the Epistle of John, the emphasis is the *abiding* propitiation. As the righteous One, He pleads and He is ever efficacious because He is the One who has removed the righteous judgment of God against men. His sacrifice is inexhaustible and eternally valid.

Propitiation is not something we must feel or experience; it is a fact to be accepted. *Relationship* is established with the eternal, righteous God the moment we receive the

Saviour. This salvation is *declared* in the Gospel of John and *explained* in the Book of Romans. Here, in the Epistle of John, he is talking about our *fellowship*. We are responsible for our sin, but *He* is the One who has made provision for us to be cleansed.

After we have accepted the Saviour, *our relationship with God never changes.* We have become the children of God for all eternity. Our standing before God never changes. We stand before Him as His redeemed children, clothed in all the righteousness of Christ Jesus (II Cor. 5:21). However, *our fellowship with Him does change.* We may be in fellowship with God today and may fail Him tomorrow. In His wonderful grace He has made provision for this failure. Christ is our Advocate with the Father. He pleads our cause on the ground of His all-sufficient sacrifice for our sin (I John 4:9,10).

God has so graciously and wondrously manifested His love for us. Do you realize that we have been redeemed, not primarily that we might change the world, but that we might *walk in fellowship with God?* This is the great longing of His heart. Abraham walked with God as a friend. He is called the "friend of God" in II Chronicles 20:7; Isaiah 41:8; James 2:23. What did he do for the world? He pleaded with God for men (Gen. 18:23-33 and Gen. 20:17,18).

Just so, when we walk with God, we have weapons so powerful that the armies of the earth cannot withstand them. We have the Word of God, which is the sword of the Spirit (Eph. 6:17). We have the privilege of "praying always with all prayer and supplication in the Spirit, and watching thereunto with all perseverance and supplication for all saints" (Eph. 6:18).

Fellowshiping with God is simply walking with Him whatever and wherever our jobs may be. It is magnifying Him in all that we do. Won't you rejoice today that God is completely satisfied with the work of His Son? Won't you revel in the love of the Saviour and enjoy his fellowship?

THE EVIDENCE OF FELLOWSHIP WITH GOD

There is a question that needs to be answered. How can I know when I am in fellowship with this God who is light, who is absolute in holiness, in whom is no darkness at all? Feelings and ecstatic experiences are transient and unreliable. We must turn to the Word of God to find the answer. We find that there are three things that characterize the life of a Christian when he is really walking in fellowship with God.

1. The first evidence is obedience to His Word.

> **And hereby we do know that we know him, if we keep his commandments.**
>
> **He that saith, I know him, and keepeth not his commandments, is a liar, and the truth is not in him.**
>
> **But whoso keepeth his word, in him verily is the love of God perfected: hereby know we that we are in him (I John 2:3-5).**

Here we have a statement of *experiential* knowledge. That is to say, our experience in fellowship with God is tested. If our relationship to God is a real relationship and if it is a personal fellowship with God who is light, then it will be manifested by obedience to His Word. In fact, perfect obedience is the evidence of a perfect love for Him. "He that hath my commandments, and keepeth them, he it is that loveth me ... If a man love me, he will keep my words: and my Father will love him, and we will come unto him, and make our abode with him" (John 14:21,23).

Our perfect example in this is the Lord Jesus Christ.

"But that the world may know that I love the Father; and as the Father gave me commandment, even so I do" (John 14:31).

"For I do always those things that please him" (John 8:29).

"My meat is to do the will of him that sent me, and to finish his work" (John 4:34). This was the great desire of the heart of Christ.

We must admit that even though we want to obey the Word of God, we fail so often. God knows, and we all recognize, that we are living in bodies that are frail and that fail God. Sin comes to us through the lust of the flesh, the lust of the eyes, and the pride of life. We see things, we hear things, we do things, we desire things that break our fellowship with God. Words pop out of our mouth without any thinking, and we are amazed at what we said. We are amazed at some of the things we do because we do not want to do them.

The unsaved man, the one who is not a Christian, does not feel that way. The man of the world does what *he wants to do.* He has no desire for the Word of God. He has no desire to obey the Word of God. We who are Christians have a yearning for the fellowship of God. We *want* to serve the Lord. We *want* to do the Lord's will. We *want* to be found obedient to Him. That very thing, my friend, is one of the evidences that we belong to Him. "Whoso keepth his word, in him verily is the love of God perfected: hereby know we that we are in him."

When we accept the Saviour, there is planted in our hearts a great desire for God, for His fellowship, for His Word. Even though we are weak and often fail, yet there is in our hearts the great desire to do the will of God. "His delight is in the law of the LORD; and in his law doth he meditate day and night" (Psa. 1:2). If obedience to the Word of God is not the desire of your heart, then, my friend, I would like to ask you a question. Have you really accepted Christ as your personal Saviour? Have you come into right relationship with Him?

Obedience to His Word is the measure of our love for Christ and is also the evidence of our fellowship and union with Him. This is experiential knowledge, something we know. It is not a theory, nor a doctrine, nor some theology which men may teach, but it is a reality in our own life. God has provided the possibility of personal, intimate fellowship with Himself. This is why He sent His Son. He redeemed man, and He removed the barrier between man and God, so that man could have a relationship with God and also have intimate fellowship with Him. It is possible for a Christian on earth to walk in fellowship with God day by day, hour by hour, moment by moment. In fact, the whole Gospel of Luke tells us how Jesus, *as a man,* walked in continual moment by moment fellowship with His Father. This fellowship can also be ours. What is the evidence of such fellowship? Obedience to His Word!

Is this what you *want* to do?

2. The second evidence of fellowship with God is submission to His will.

> He that saith he abideth in him ought himself also so to walk, even as he walked.
>
> Brethren, I write no new commandment unto you, but an old commandment which ye had from the beginning. The old commandment is the word which ye have heard from the beginning.
>
> Again, a new commandment I write unto you, which thing is true in him and in you: because the darkness is past, and the true light now shineth (I John 2:6-8).

Allow me to paraphrase verse 6: "He who confesses or says that he is in fellowship with God ought to walk even as Christ walked." Lest someone should misunderstand what John is writing, let me state that he does not say that if we are abiding in Him, we will do the same things that He did. He does not say that! He does say that we will walk as He walked.

The "old commandment" in verse seven is found in John 13 where Jesus says, "A new commandment I give unto you, That ye love one another; as I have loved you, that ye also love one another. By this shall all men know that ye are my disciples, if ye have love one to another (John 13:34,35).

This was a "new commandment" which He gave them while He walked among them, but now it has become the "old commandment." Then what is the "new commandment" which John mentions in verse six? It is absolute submission to the will of the Father. If I say that I am in fellowship with God, then I will walk even as He walked. And how did He walk? That which characterized the life of Jesus as He walked a Man among men was *His absolute submission to the will of His Father.*

This submission to the Father's will was prophesied in the Psalms. "Sacrifice and offering thou didst not desire; mine ears hast thou opened: burnt-offering and sin-offering hast thou not required. Then said I, Lo, I come: in the volume of the book it is written of me, I delight to do thy will, O my God: yea, thy law is within my heart" (Psa. 40:6-8). This is repeated in Hebrews 10:5-10 where twice we read, "Lo, I come to do thy will, O God." You cannot find a time in the life of our Lord Jesus Christ when He was not in absolute submission to His Father.

When our Lord became 12 years of age, Joseph and Mary took Him to Jerusalem into the temple before God so that He might take His place as a son under the law. This was their custom as the law demanded. After this, Jesus was personally responsible to God for His own life. As Joseph and Mary were returning to Nazareth, they missed Jesus and returned to Jerusalem to find Him. They found Him in the midst of the doctors, confounding those doctors in the temple. When they told Jesus they had been looking all over for Him, He answered, "How is it that ye sought me; wist ye not that I must be about my Father's business?" (Luke 2:49). As a son under the law, He was responsible to be obedient and submissive to His Father's will.

Notice these words of our Lord:

"My meat is to do the will of him that sent me, and to finish his work" (John 4:34).

"For I came down from heaven, not to do mine own will, but the will of him that sent me" (John 6:38).

"And he that sent me is with me: the Father hath not left me alone; for I do always those things that please him" (John 8:29).

"Nevertheless not as I will, but as thou wilt" (Matt. 26:39).

"Jesus knowing that the Father had given all things into his hands, and that he was come from God, and went to God . . . " (John 13:3). The Father had utter confidence in the Son, trusting that He would go through and do the work that He was supposed to do.

"I have glorified thee on the earth: I have finished the work which thou gavest me to do" (John 17:4).

"It is finished" (John 19:30).

He had completed everything that was in the Father's will and purpose for Him to do. That which characterized the life of our Saviour was complete submission to the will of His Father.

When we walk in fellowship with God, there will be in us, that same submission to the will of our Father. Again I ask, how can we know the will of our Father, how can we be obedient to His Word, unless we stay in the Word of God? How can we know the purpose of God for our lives unless we live in the Word of God where it is revealed to us? We do not know the will of God by some experience. We find the will of God, we find the purpose of God for our lives, we find the desire of God for us, in the Word of God. We must go to the Word of God! The more we read it, the more we hide the Word in our minds and in our hearts, the greater will be our desire to be obedient to His Word and to be submissive to His will. When this is true, He will have more delight in us, and we will have more fulness of joy in Him.

Profession carries with it an obligation. Divine fellowship results in a corresponding action. We will *walk as He walked.* And when we walk as He walked, we will *love as He loved.* Isn't that going too far? What did He say? "That ye love one another; as I have loved you, that ye also love one another. By this shall all men know that ye are my disciples, if ye have love one to another" (John 13:34,35).

We are to *forgive as He has forgiven.* But He forgave everything! That's right. And we are to forgive everything. "And be ye kind one to another, tenderhearted, forgiving one another, even as God for Christ's sake hath forgiven you" (Eph. 4:32). "Forbearing one another, and forgiving one another, if any man have a quarrel against any: even as Christ forgave you, so also do ye" (Col. 3:13).

We are to *serve as He served.* "As thou hast sent me into the world, even so have I also sent them into the world. And for their sakes I sanctify myself, that they also might be santified through the truth" (John 17:18,19). "Peace be unto you: as my Father hath sent me, even so send I you" (John 20:21).

Here is a life to be lived. We are not under the law of the Ten Commandments, nor are we under the Sermon on the Mount. We are on a higher plane. The Ten Commandments and the Sermon on the Mount are *law.* The Sermon on the Mount sets forth the spirit of the law. Hating a brother without a cause is equal to murder. Lusting after a woman is adultery in the heart. This is the spirit of the law. *We have a higher walk.* We are to walk as He walked, love as He loved, forgive as He has forgiven, serve as He served. This is a supernatural life. It can be lived only by Christ living in us. If we say that we are abiding in Him, that we are walking in fellowship with Him, then we will walk as He walked in obedience and in submission to the will of the Father.

After His resurrection, Jesus sent forth His disciples to bear testimony to the world, to reveal something of the character and heart and love and grace and tenderness and compassion of God. How else can the world know Him unless we walk as He walked, love as He loved, forgive as He has forgiven, and serve as He served?

If we desire to have Christ live this supernatural life through us, then there is one more wonderful thing which we must do. We are to *pray as He prayed*. Will you please open your Bible to John 16 and read the entire passage from verse 23 to verse 28. We will note that Jesus said to His disciples, "At that day ye shall ask in my name: and I say not unto you, that I will pray the Father for you: For the Father himself loveth you, because ye have loved me, and have believed that I came out from God" (John 16:26,27). He is saying, "I am giving you the same rights that I have. Just as I come into the presence of My Father and make My needs known, so can you, because you love Me." What a blessed privilege!

To walk as He walked is something we cannot accomplish in our own strength. It is supernatural. It is impossible for a man to imitate Christ. This is the very reason He has given us the Word of God and He has given us the Spirit of God who indwells us. It is impossible for the man of the world to live the Christian life. And it is impossible for us, apart from Him. The only way this life is possible is by yielding our lives to God so that *He might live His life through us.* "I am crucified with Christ: nevertheless I live; yet not I, but Christ liveth in me: and the life which I now live in the flesh I live by the faith of the Son of God, who loved me, and gave himself for me" (Gal. 2:20). "But if the Spirit of him that raised up Jesus from the dead dwell in you, he that raised up Christ from the dead shall also quicken your mortal bodies by his Spirit that dwelleth in you" (Rom. 8:11).

So it is possible for us to live the life that He wants us to live. When we walk in fellowship with God, there will be that evidence. Not by some crisis experience! Not by miracles! Not by spiritual gifts! Spiritual gifts are not a sign of spirituality. A person can have all the gifts of the Spirit and still be carnal. One needs only to read the Book of Corinthians to find this. In chapter 14 we read that they had all the gifts of the Spirit, yet in I Corinthians 3:1-4 Paul says four times, "Ye are carnal." Just because one has had some great experience does not mean that person is spiritual. Spirituality is evident by obedience to the Word of God and submission to the will of God.

3. The third evidence of fellowship with God is love for the brethren.

> He that saith he is in the light, and hateth his brother, is in darkness even until now.
>
> He that loveth his brother abideth in the light, and there is none occasion of stumbling in him.
>
> But he that hateth his brother is in darkness, and walketh in darkness, and knoweth not whither he goeth, because that darkness hath blinded his eyes (I John 2:9-11).

Walking in love for the brethren is an indication that we are walking in fellowship with the living God. In Colossians 1:13 we read that God has "delivered us from the power of darkness, and hath translated us into the kingdom of his dear Son." If I am walking in that light, if I really know the Lord, then it will be manifested by love for the brethren. This love for God's people is not something that *we* can produce but it is made possible and made known by our union with *Him,* "because the love of God is shed abroad in our hearts by the Holy Ghost which is given unto us" (Romans 5:5). In other words, divine love is in the heart of every Christian. As we yield ourselves to Him, there will be evidence of that love one for another.

Allow me to show a contrast here. You will notice there are three things said about the believer. He *walks* in the light as He is in the light (I John 1:7). He *is in* the light (I John 2:9) and he *abides* in the light (I John 2:10). Love is the evidence of *where* he lives. There are also three things stated about the unbeliever and darkness. The unbeliever *is in* darkness, he *walks* in darkness, and darkness has *blinded* his eyes (I John 2:11).

Our love for our brother, in spite of his faults, manifests that we are in the light and not in the dark. It is easy to love those who love us. Unfortunately, when another Christian fails, our problem is that we sit as judges and critics, and then *we* are not very lovable. We ought to love the brother, in spite of his failure, and seek to help him because we love him. "Brethren, if a man be overtaken in a fault, ye which are spiritual, restore such an one in the spirit of meekness; considering thyself, lest thou also be tempted" (Gal. 6:1).

A fellow Christian may be in trouble, in failure, out of fellowship with God. He may be bitter or just plain "ornery." How are we going to bring him out of it if we do not love him? This does not mean that we condone sin. It does mean that we should manifest love. When we seek to restore such an one, it should not be with a censorious and critical spirit, but rather in love. One of the tragedies of the present time is that so many churches (I say this very sadly) have been split and shattered because of lack of love one for another. One who boasts about being evangelical, about loving the Saviour, about loving truth and sound doctrine, is very inconsistent if he hates his brother. The inevitable mark of walking in fellowship with God who is light is love for the brethren. "By this shall all men know that ye are my disciples, if ye have love one to another" (John 13:35).

Is it not wonderful that the Lord's love for us never changes? Our frailty and failure never affect His love for us. God grant that we shall manifest the same spirit to those who belong to the Saviour. May obedience to His Word, submission to His will, and love for the brethren characterize our lives.

THE PLACE OF THE FELLOWSHIP

I write unto you, little children, because your sins are forgiven you for his name's sake (I John 2:12).

We find that the place of the fellowship is in the family. In this verse, the Greek word for children is "teknia" which means the "born ones" and includes *the whole family of God.* The only way we can be in the family of God is by the new birth (John 1:12,13; I Pet. 1:23). To those who are in the family John says, "I write unto you, teknia (born ones), because your sins are forgiven you for his name's sake." Forgiveness is for the whole family! We are speaking here of something that is true for every believer. This complete, perfect, and permanent pardon for every believer is based on the grace of God.

"In whom we have redemption through his blood, the forgiveness of sins, ACCORDING TO THE RICHES OF HIS GRACE" (Eph. 1:7).

"And be ye kind one to another, tenderhearted, forgiving one another, even as God FOR CHRIST'S SAKE hath forgiven you" (Eph. 4:32).

"I write unto you, little children, because your sins are forgiven you FOR HIS NAME'S SAKE" (I John 2:12).

How wonderful it is to have this blessed assurance, to know that the moment we come to the Saviour we have forgiveness of sins and we receive a pardon that is eternal. We are accepted in the Beloved. We are members of the family of God.

John goes on to speak of three kinds of people in the family of God. There are the fathers, the young men, and the babies. They have all been born into the family, but they are not all at the same stage of maturity. They have not all attained the same spiritual growth. He has something to say to each of them. He speaks first to the fathers.

1. The declaration to the fathers.

> I write unto you, fathers, because ye have known him that is from the beginning (I John 2:13).

> I have written unto you, fathers, because ye have known him that is from the beginning (I John 2:14).

He is not talking here about a person who has led someone else to Christ. Paul did use the word "father" with that meaning when he wrote to the Corinthian church that they had many teachers but one father (I Cor. 4:15). In a sense, we become spiritual fathers to people when we lead them to the Saviour and build them up in Christ. But that is not the meaning here. He is talking about spiritual growth. They are fathers in the faith and they are mature spiritually.

You will notice that there is no word of exhortation concerning walk or doctrine given to the fathers. He simply says, "I write unto you fathers, because you have known Him." This is *experiential knowledge.* They are fathers because of their experience in Christ. These are the ones who know intimately the Incarnate Word of God. They have gone through the tests and trials and afflictions of life, and yet, in spite of it all, *they are fully satisfied with Christ.* The world has no more pull on them. The flesh is kept in subjection. They know how to walk before God. If they fail, they know what to do. They confess their sin to God, are forgiven and cleansed, and go on in perfect fellowship with Him. This is the mature, the truly spiritual Christian.

If the apostle had no admonition to the fathers, neither do I. If you believe that you are a father, that you are mature in faith and in spiritual life, that you know sound doctrine, that you know where you stand, then you can say with Paul: "I know whom I have believed, and am persuaded that he is able to keep that which I have committed unto him against that day" (II Tim. 1:12). "Being confident of this very thing, that he which hath begun a good work in you will perform it until the day of Jesus Christ" (Phil. 1:6).

The great yearning of the heart of God is that His people may be absolutely, perfectly satisfied with the Saviour. It is possible for a Christian to so walk with God, to be so in love with the Saviour, to so know the Word of God, that the one desire of his heart is to please Him. The circumstances, trials, afflictions, troubles, disappointments, and sorrows of life do not disturb the deep-seated peace of the mature Christian because he knows the Lord is with him. He knows that the Lord will never leave him, that He knows all the circumstances, and that He is the God over all circumstances. He is perfectly satisfied to trust Him for every moment of every day, to know His way, and to walk in it. His great joy is to live in fellowship with his Lord. The eleventh chapter of Hebrews teaches us that God has given us faith, not to transform the world, but *to walk with Him.*

Are you a mature Christian? Do you know what it means to walk with God? This is our desire for each one of you.

2. The address to the young men.

I write unto you, young men, because ye have overcome the wicked one (I John 2:13).

I have written unto you, young men, because ye are strong, and the word of God abideth in you, and ye have overcome the wicked one.

Love not the world, neither the things that are in the world. If any man love the world, the love of the Father is not in him.

For all that is in the world, the lust of the flesh, and the lust of the eyes, and the pride of life, is not of the Father, but is of the world.

> **And the world passeth away, and the lust thereof:**
> **but he that doeth the will of God abideth for ever**
> **(I John 2:14-17).**

The young men are the believers in conflict. Three things are said about them. *They are strong.* That is, they have spiritual power and courage of faith and purpose. They have conviction and are not tossed about by every wind of doctrine. They have a real purpose in life.

The reason they are strong is because *the Word of God is abiding in them.* It is their daily food. It is the sword by which they overcome the Wicked One. The third statement John makes concerning them is that *they have overcome the wicked one.* There is no possibility of victory over the enemy apart from the Word of God. We, too, can be strong when we use the only aggressive weapon that God has given us—the Word of God abiding in us.

In Matthew 4 and Luke 4 we find the story of our Saviour in the wilderness, being led there of the Spirit to be tempted of the devil. Satan approached Him with testing concerning the *grace of God,* the *Word of God,* and the *Person of God.* You will remember that the Lord answered, "It is written!" "It is written!" "It is written!" If we are to have victory over the enemy, we must be able to say, "It is written!" My Christian friend, may I say very solemnly that it is not possible to live the Christian life without a knowledge of the Word of God. We must spend time in His Word to know the Saviour whom we trust, the One who is our Lord and who gives us the victory.

In verses 15-17 we find that *the young men have another enemy—the world!* John gives a strong exhortation concerning this. Let us read those verses again:

> **Love not the world, neither the things that are in**
> **the world. If any man love the world, the love of**
> **the Father is not in him.**

> For all that is in the world, the lust of the flesh,
> and the lust of the eyes, and the pride of life, is not
> of the Father, but is of the world.
>
> And the world passeth away, and the lust thereof;
> but he that doeth the will of God abideth for ever
> (I John 2:15-17).

What is meant here by the world? It is a system, an economic, social, political, religious system. It started with Cain who went out from the presence of the Lord and built a city (Gen. 4). His purpose was to make the earth a beautiful place to live in—*without God.* This is still true today. Let us always remember that the world is our enemy. There is a tremendous barrier between God the Father and the world.

The world appeals to us through three avenues: the lust of the flesh, the lust of the eyes, and the pride of life. This is always true. In Genesis, chapter three, we find that Satan tempted Adam and Eve these three ways. He questioned the *love of God* by implying that God was withholding something good from them in forbidding them to eat of the tree of the knowledge of good and evil. He caused them to doubt the *Word of God* when he told them they would not die. Then he attacked the *Person of God* by saying they would be like gods, knowing good and evil. He tempted them in the lust of the flesh, the lust of the eyes, and the pride of life.

"And when the woman saw that the tree was good for food, and that it was pleasant to the eyes, and a tree to be desired to make one wise, she took of the fruit thereof, and did eat, and gave also unto her husband with her; and he did eat" (Gen. 3:6). Her pride was manifest because she desired to be as God. She rebelled against the law and character of God. She was disobedient to the Word of God. In deliberately disobeying, she sinned and became alienated from God.

Satan used the same approaches when he tempted our Lord in the wilderness. He will approach *you* in the same way. He has not changed his methods of seeking to win men away from devotion to the Saviour and from a walk in the purpose and will of Christ. He wants to defeat the purpose of God in *your* life. He comes in the lust of the flesh, the lust of the eyes, and the pride of life.

The worst of the three is pride. Pride was the cause of Satan's downfall. *Pride is the root sin.* The thing that oftentimes keeps us from doing that which God wants us to do is pride. But let us remember that, apart from what we have in Christ, we have nothing of which we can be proud. "For I know that in me (that is, in my flesh,) dwelleth no good thing" (Rom. 7:18). If we have any gifts or talents, let us thank God for them. He is the Giver. We are the recipients.

So we see that we have three implacable enemies: the world, the flesh, and the devil. Sometimes we think that our lives should be easy after we have committed ourselves to the Lord. Then we find that we have more tests and trials than before we became Christians. That is to be expected! Before we became Christians, we did not have any opposition from the world, the flesh, and the devil, because we lived without any responsiblity to God. Now that we are Christians, our lives have been changed. We are in *His* family. We are indwelt by the Holy Spirit. We want to do His will. Our citizenship is in heaven, from whence we look for our Saviour. We are occupied with Him. Our responsibility is to love Him and serve Him and tell others about Him. We can expect to be attacked by the enemy who is always in opposition to God and to those who desire to live for Him.

Every believer is engaged in a warfare. Paul writes of this in Ephesians 6:10-18. Our fight is against Satan and all his cohorts, all the rulers of the darkness of this world. He speaks not only of our enemy, but also of the provision we have against him. He exhorts us to put on the whole armour of God. "Stand therefore, having your loins girt about with truth, and having on the breastplate of righteousness; and your feet shod with the preparation of the gospel of peace; above all, taking the shield of faith, wherewith ye shall be able to quench all the fiery darts of the wicked. And take the helmet of salvation, and the sword of the Spirit, which is the word of God: Praying always with all prayer and supplication in the Spirit, and watching . . . " (Eph. 6:14-18).

May I suggest a study that reveals the exactness and perfection of Scripture concerning our enemies and the provision made for us.

It is the *Father* who is in opposition to the *world* (I John 2:15). In the seventeeth chapter of the Gospel of John, our Saviour is talking to the Father concerning His own and He mentions the "world" 19 times. Then He prays, "I pray not that thou shouldest take them out of the world, but that thou shouldest keep them from the evil. They are not of the world, even as I am not of the world" (John 17:15,16).

It is the *Spirit* who is in opposition to the *flesh* (Gal. 5:16,25; Rom. 8:12,13).

It is *Christ* who is in opposition to *Satan,* or antichrist (I John 3:8; Heb. 2:14, 15; I John 4:2, 3).

Every provision has been made for us. We know that the whole world system of which we have been speaking is under the judgment of God. We who are in the family of God have been delivered, not only from judgment, but also from the power of Satan and from the present evil world (Gal. 1:3,4; Gal. 6:14). It is wonderful to know that between the believer and the world stands the cross of Christ. Because this is true, we have a special responsibility: "Love not the world, neither the things that are in the world . . . the world passeth away, and the lust thereof: but he that doeth the will of God abideth for ever" (I John 2:15,17).

The world and its lust do not endure. Let me emphasize again that the world is under the judgment of God, and Christians have been delivered from the world. Why should we waste our time on passing, transient things when we can know the joys and blessings of fellowship with the One who is eternal? How many Christians are frittering away their time with things that perish with the using, when they could be occupied with eternal glories!

My friend, when our hearts are occupied with Him, we can know the peace of God, the rest of heart that is found only in Him. We can experience His joy in the midst of suffering, His comfort in sorrow. It is an amazing thing that the eternal, omnipotent God has made provision for us to walk with Him. Let us not let anything rob us of this intimacy and fellowship.

There can be only one supreme object of moral devotion. It will be either the world or the Father.

Where is the devotion of your heart? He loves *you* and has a special plan and purpose for *you.* May your heart be set upon Him so that He can lead you and bless you and use you.

3. The instruction to the little children.

The apostle now writes to the last group in the family of God, the little children. The Greek word here is "paidia" which means "the inexperienced ones" or, let me use the term, the little babies.

> I write unto you, little children, because ye have known the Father (I John 2:13).
>
> Little children, it is the last time: and as ye have heard that antichrist shall come, even now are there many antichrists; whereby we know that it is the last time.
>
> They went out from us, but they were not of us; for if they had been of us, they would no doubt have continued with us: but they went out, that they might be made manifest that they were not all of us (I John 2:18, 19).

The enemy of the young men is the world, and the enemy of the babes in Christ is the false teacher. In the early church the false teachers manifested themselves by denying the Incarnate Word of God. In chapter 4, verses 2 and 3, we read that the spirit of antichrist is the denial of the person of our Saviour. This is stated here in chapter 2, verses 21-26, in more detail. These seducers do not teach that Jesus is the Christ nor that this Jesus of Nazareth is God manifest in the flesh.

The deity of Jesus was the issue when our Lord stood before the high priest in Matthew 26. The high priest said to our Lord, "I adjure thee by the living God, that thou tell us whether thou be the Christ, the Son of God. Jesus saith unto him, Thou hast said: nevertheless I say unto you, Hereafter shall ye see the Son of man sitting on the right hand of power, and coming in the clouds of heaven" (Matt. 26:63,64). The high priest had put our Lord under oath and when he did that, our Lord said in effect, "That is true. I am the Christ, the Son of God. Not only that, but I am the One who is going to fulfill Daniel chapter seven, for the Messiah is going to come in the clouds of heaven." You will remember that our Lord spoke of this to His disciples in Matthew 16:27,28, Matthew 24:30, and Matthew 25:31-46.

The spirit of antichrist denies all that Jesus Christ claimed to be and to do. This is the issue brought to us in the second and third Epistles of John. The ones they were to exclude from the fellowship were those who denied the Incarnate Word of God. It was evident who they were, and it was manifest that they did not belong in the church of Jesus Christ. In the twentieth century church, those who *believe* that Jesus Christ is the Incarnate Word of God are sometimes asked to leave. My, what a contrast to the first century church! We see it clearly set before us here. When a person or a church denies that Jesus of Nazareth is the Son of God, that person or church has the spirit of antichrist, and we are told to have nothing to do with them. I am not trying to be hard or severe. I am telling you what the Word of God has to say.

The babes in Christ are warned to beware of these false teachers. We know that the various cults today, with their false doctrines, seek out inexperienced Christians. They work on those who are untaught and who know little of the Word of God. They may come to your door with a Bible under their arm, but the purpose is to detract from the glorious person of Christ, the Incarnate Word of God. They deny the physical resurrection of Christ, who died to put away our sin and was raised again from the dead by the glory of the Father. We find the same thing on the mission field. The cults do not go to the unsaved, the pagans, and idolators. They go to those who are babes in Christ, who know the Saviour but are untaught, and try to lead them astray.

The important advice to the babes in Christ is to feed on the Word of God. One does not feed a baby T-bone steak, but milk. This is stated in Hebrews 5:12-14. Babies need milk to grow. "As newborn babes, desire the sincere milk of the word, that ye may grow thereby" (I Pet. 2:2).

Babes in Christ, you cannot stand for God in this world unless you are nourished by the Word of God. You may say, "Mr. Mitchell, you always come back to that." That's right! I do, because you cannot grow apart from the Word of God. You cannot overcome the enemy apart from the Word of God. You cannot walk before God in fellowship with Him apart from His Word.

Let us be like the psalmist. "His delight is in the law of the LORD; and in his law doth he meditate day and night" (Psa. 1:2). Let us heed the exhortation of the apostle, "Let the word of Christ dwell in you richly" (Col. 3:16). Remember that God is the faithful One. Jesus assures us that the Spirit of God will use His Word in our lives. "The words that I speak unto you, they are spirit, and they are life" (John 6:63). "Now ye are clean through the word which I have spoken unto you" (John 15:3).

So you see that the babes in Christ do not need admonition on how to walk as much as warning concerning false teachers. They are in the family. They have forgiveness. They know the Father. The exhortation to them is to be occupied with the Incarnate Word of God. The reason is that it is the last time and there are many antichristian forces in the world.

In verses 22 and 23 John tells us that the one who loves the Saviour will acknowledge both the Father and the Son. Be careful about someone who comes to you with new truth. The Word of God was given to us and completed in the first century. The Son of God has been revealed. The revelation of God in His purposes and plans has been fully given.

If you are a babe in Christ, seek daily to know what God has revealed in His Word. May I encourage you to read it even though there is much you may not understand. Read it and read it and reread it, and the Lord will reveal Himself to you.

The apostle continues by giving encouragement to these babes in Christ, the little children of the family of God. The first of these encouragements is the *Holy Spirit who is indwelling them.*

> But ye have an unction from the Holy One, and ye know all things (I John 2:20).

> But the anointing which ye have received of him abideth in you, and ye need not that any man teach you: but as the same anointing teacheth you of all things, and is truth, and is no lie, and even as it hath taught you, ye shall abide in him (I John 2:27).

John does not mean here that we are not to have teachers, for God has given gifted men to teach the Word of God (Eph. 4:11-13). We can know these men from the false teachers because they make Jesus Christ, the Incarnate Word of God, the center of attraction. He does mean that because the Spirit of God, who is the author of Scripture, indwells every believer, He will lead and guide into all truth and keep us from that which is false (John 16:13). He also enables us to compare spiritual things with spiritual (I Cor. 2:13). We are not to believe everything we hear, but we are to prove all things, and we must prove them by the Word of God.

The second encouragement is that we have the *Word of God* by which to prove all things.

> I have not written unto you because ye know not the truth, but because ye know it, and that no lie is of the truth.
>
> Who is a liar but he that denieth that Jesus is the Christ? He is antichrist, that denieth the Father and the Son.
>
> Whosoever denieth the Son, the same hath not the Father: (but) he that acknowledgeth the Son hath the Father also.
>
> Let that therefore abide in you which ye have heard from the beginning. If that which ye have heard from the beginning shall remain in you, ye also shall continue in the Son, and in the Father.
>
> And this is the promise that he hath promised us, even eternal life.
>
> These things have I written unto you concerning them that seduce you (I John 2:21-26).

One is ever amazed at how little God's people know of the Word of God, of the purpose of God for their lives and for the church. There are comparatively few who lovingly and diligently study the Scriptures. The result is that many, although they have been saved for 30 or 40 or 50 years, are still babes in Christ. Babyhood is wonderful in only one place and that is in babies. Everyone of us who belongs to the family of God has the indwelling Spirit to teach us how to know the Word of God and how to walk before Him in the path that He has for us. You will remember Paul's admonition to Timothy: "Continue thou in the things which thou hast learned and hast been assured of, knowing of whom thou hast learned them; and that from a child thou hast known the holy scriptures, which are able to make thee wise unto salvation through faith which is in Christ Jesus" (II Tim. 3:14,15).

This is God's weapon for us. The Word of God is unchanging. It is forever settled in heaven (Psa. 119:89). It will keep us steady in times of trial and testing as we contend with opposition, false doctrine, and the pull of the world. Stay in the Word. Meditate upon these things. Give yourself wholly to them.

The third encouragement is the *promise of His coming.* Actually, this encouragement is not for the babes only but for the whole family of God, because the Greek word used here is the same one which was in verse 12, "teknia," which means the "born ones."

> **And now, little children, abide in him; that, when he shall appear, we may have confidence, and not be ashamed before him at his coming (I John 2:28).**

Abiding in Him should be the normal Christian experience. In I John 3:24 we find that to abide in Him is to obey Him. Perhaps you thought that abiding in Christ means having fellowship with God. That is true. But it is when we obey the Word of God that we are in fellowship with Him. Our sins have been forgiven, the Spirit of God indwells us, we have His Word, we are partners with Him, we are one with Him. Then let us obey His Word and fully enjoy fellowship with Him. John tells us here that we should stay in fellowship with Him, so that, when He shall appear, we may have confidence and not be ashamed before Him at His coming.

We could look at this verse in several ways. Was John, as an apostle of Christ, going to be ashamed of his children who were not walking with God? This could be the meaning, and I could appreciate that point of view. A pastor comes before God in behalf of some of those whom he has led to the Saviour and then finds that they are not walking orderly and are not bringing honor to the Lord. The world has come into their lives; the flesh with its weakness has taken over. If the Lord should come, the pastor would wonder, "Where have I failed these dear people? In instruction? In encouragement?" So it could be that John is saying that if the Lord should come and you are not walking in fellowship with Him, then we Apostles, we who have given you the revelation of our wonderful Saviour, would be ashamed.

However, I am inclined to believe it is a personal matter. The whole family of God, individually and collectively, will have confidence and will come into His presence with a boldness of speech and not be ashamed before Him at His coming. I have thought a good deal about this. Is it possible that there are going to be some who are going to be taken up to be with the Lord who are going to be ashamed when they stand in His presence? My friend, if the Lord Jesus should come for His own today, and He may, would you be ashamed of what you are doing? Would you be ashamed of some of the things you have said? Would you be ashamed of some of the plans you are making? This verse is very practical and heart searching.

"And God shall wipe away all tears from their eyes" (Rev. 21:4). I wonder if this will be because some Christians will be ashamed before Him at His coming. The translation of the church is on the ground of grace. But the question here is: Will we be found abiding in fellowship with Him?

God is faithful to everyone who has put his trust in Him. He is faithful to the strong and the weak ones, to the mature in Christ and the babes in Christ. He gives us divine life when we accept Him. Then He makes provision for us to experience and enjoy that divine life and to live in continual fellowship with Him. The Spirit of God comes to indwell us and to plead our cause before Christ. He has given us the Word of God in our hands to read so that we might be cleansed through the Word and receive light from it. Christ, the Lord of Glory, pleads our cause before the Father. What a provision God has made for us!

This 28th verse is a great encouragement to all of us. The same thought is in Hebrews 10:37: "He that shall come will come, and will not tarry." It is an amazing thing that when we stand before God, we will stand before Him in all the beauty and righteousness of Christ. In view of this, we are encouraged to abide in Him, to walk in fellowship with Him, to obey Him, so that we shall not be ashamed before Him at His coming.

Yesterday you may have had a wonderful experience with the Lord. That is marvellous. But that is past, my friend. What about today? The great yearning of the heart of God is for your fellowship today, wherever you are.

And now, little children, abide in Him!

FELLOWSHIP
WITH GOD
WHO IS RIGHTEOUS

> If ye know that he is righteous, ye know that every one that doeth righteousness is born of him (I John 2:29).

We have come to the second great division of the Epistle and we learn that God is righteous. He is righteous in every thing He does, which means that He *always* does the right thing.

We find some people sitting in judgment on God, asking why God permits certain things to happen in the earth. They mention war, bloodshed, and sorrow and ask why God does not step into the scene. My friend, may I say to you, do not sit in judgment on God! Dare we infer that we are more righteous than God? Dare we infer that we are more loving or more merciful than God? God is not dealing with nations today. God is dealing with men and women everywhere, wherever He finds them. If God were dealing with nations today, the wrath of God would be upon them for their sins, their corruption, and their opposition to Him. God is righteous, and everything He does is right. I may not understand all that He does. That does not alter the fact. Abraham, as he pleaded for the cities of Sodom and Gomorrah, could say, "Shall not the Judge of all the earth do right?" (Gen. 18:25).

Here, then, is the revelation that God is righteous. *The requirement for fellowship with a righteous God, of course, is righteousness.*

A believer may be discouraged to find that after a profession of faith he still sins. We discussed this at the end of the first chapter and the beginning of the second chapter. God has made provision for cleansing and forgiving the sins of His people. Yet it is true that a *practical* righteousness certainly must be consistent in one who is in fellowship with a righteous God. If we claim to be in fellowship with a God who is righteous, then our lives will be righteous. At least there will be evidence of practical righteousness which will be consistent with the God whom we love and serve and with whom we walk.

This is not to be confused with *imputed* righteousness, which means to "be found in him, not having mine own righteousness, which is of the law, but that which is through faith of Christ, the righteousness which is of God by faith" (Phil. 3:9).

". . But of him are ye in Christ Jesus, who of God is made unto us . . . righteousness" (I Cor. 1:30).

"For Christ is the end of the law for righteousness to every one that believeth" (Rom. 10:4).

"For he hath made him to be sin for us, who knew no sin; that we might be made the righteousness of God in him" (II Cor. 5:21).

Romans 1:16,17 states that the gospel is the revelation of the righteousness of God. Romans 3:21-31, that basic passage on justification by faith, declares that God may be just (righteous) and the justifier of him that believeth in Jesus. When Jesus Christ died on the cross, He made it possible for God to seek unrighteous, sinful people and pronounce them righteous. Remember that sin pays wages, and God executes the penalty. How can we be freed? How can *God be freed* so that He can pronounce proven sinners to be righteous? When Christ died on the cross, He *satisfied the righteous character of God* and freed God to be able to pronounce righteous those sinners who believe on His Son. This is an imputed righteousness.

Since we are in Christ Jesus, we are made the righteousness of God in Him. Such a position in Christ will also be evident in our walk. If we claim to be the children of a righteous God, then our lives ought to manifest something of that righteousness. The righteousness which we have in Christ is a divine righteousness and is able to stand the test of the holy, righteous character of God. An unsaved person, one who is born and shapen in iniquity, cannot manifest righteousness. But the person who accepts the Saviour becomes a new man or a new woman in Christ and stands before God in all the righteousness of Christ, being accepted in the beloved (II Cor. 5:17 and Eph. 1:6). This is what will be manifested as we walk in fellowship with God. Our lives will be changed. It is true that while we are still in our bodies we will have frailty and weakness and failure at times. This does not alter the fact that we stand before God in all the righteousness of Christ and that practical righteousness is the norm for one who is in fellowship with a righteous God.

Let us be very clear about this. Imputed righteousness, that is, our standing before God, is based on our relationship with God. When we manifest practical righteousness, we are proving the source of a new life. We are then revealing the fact that we belong to God. People may notice and say that we are different. Of course, we *are* different! "If any man be in Christ, he is a new creature" (II Cor. 5:17). We have the opportunity to be a channel for God to display His righteouness before men.

The danger is that we throw up our hands and say, "Well, I guess this is not for me. I fail so often." So the Apostle goes on with:

THE ENCOURAGEMENT FOR FELLOWSHIP

Behold, what manner of love the Father hath bestowed upon us, that we should be called the sons of God: therefore the world knoweth us not, because it knew him not.

Beloved, now are we the sons of God, and it doth not yet appear what we shall be: but we know that, when he shall appear, we shall be like him; for we shall see him as he is.

And every man that hath this hope in him purifieth himself, even as he is pure (I John 3:1-3).

The first thing to mark is that all Christians, the weak as well as the strong ones, are the objects of His love. Behold! Who ever heard of such a thing that sinners redeemed by the blood of Christ can become the objects of the love of God! In John 3:16 we are told the *measure* of His love. The same is true in Romans 5:8 where we read, "God commendeth his love toward us, in that, WHILE WE WERE YET SINNERS, Christ died for us." In the verse we are considering here we are dealing with the *manner* of His love. Here is an imparted, a bestowed love so great and wonderful that we are brought into relationship with Him as His children. We receive not only an imparted life, but also an imparted love.

One translation of this first verse says, "that we should be called the sons of God—and we are!" In the Gospel according to John we find this same wonderful truth of an imparted life. When a sinner accepts the Saviour, he receives a new life from God. "In him was life" (John 1:4). "As many as received him, to them gave he power to become the sons of God" (John 1:12).

In this new relationship we are partakers of the divine nature, and the imparted life which we receive is divine life. "Whereby are given unto us exceeding great and precious promises: that by these YE MIGHT BE PARTAKERS OF THE DIVINE NATURE, having escaped the corruption that is in the world through lust" (II Pet. 1:4). This is not stated to angels, nor to principalities and powers, but to redeemed sinners.

What a wonderful place His love has given us! What a nobility of position! What a place of honor, of perfect assurance, of divine relationship! We find our hearts quieted in wonder. We are the children of One who is God.

The righteous God loves us. In John 13:1, the night when Jesus was betrayed, the night that Peter denied Him, the night that all His disciples ran away and left Him, it still could be said of Jesus that "having loved His own which were in the world, He loved them unto the end." It is because of this divine love for us as His children that we can come with confidence into the presence of God and have blessed, intimate fellowship with Him. Who would not love such a Saviour? Who would not want a life of obedience and submission in fellowship with such a God?

The result of this relationship is stated in the last half of the first verse, "Therefore the world knoweth us not, because it knew him not." Did you ever stop to think that the world never understood Jesus? The Lord Jesus took His place among men and lived in the human family, but they never knew Him. He never sought wealth or fame or power. All He wanted was His Father's will. Hence the world disowned Him, cast Him out, and crucified Him.

The world still wants to carry on its program without God and without God's people. In many ways Christians are a thorn in the flesh to those leaders who wish to bring in a world dominion without God. The world is turning more and more away from God. It does not want God nor His interference with its plans and its program. When we declare that we are the children of One who is God, this world, which never knew the Saviour, will not know us either. The world had no place for Christ. The world will have no place for us.

"If the world hate you, ye know that it hated me before it hated you. If ye were of the world, the world would love his own: but because ye are not of the world, but I have chosen you out of the world, therefore the world hateth you. Remember the word that I said unto you, the servant is not greater than his lord. If they have persecuted me, they will also persecute you; if they have kept my saying, they will keep yours also" (John 15:18-20).

When we come to know the Lord, we are willing to give up even our friends for His sake. But believe me, when our friends give us up—that's different! Then we find how much pride we have. Jesus said that if a man would come after Him, he must deny himself and take up his cross daily, and follow Him (Luke 9:23). If we follow the Lord, then we should not be surprised if the world misunderstands us and has no place for us.

Our *present relationship* to God is restated in the second verse: "Beloved, now are we the sons of God" (I John 3:2). We are not waiting to become sons of God. We are the sons of God now. We will never be any closer in relationship with God, even after we have been in the glory for a thousand years. Relationship does not change. Fellowship does.

"As many as received him, to them gave he power to become the sons of God" (John 1:12).

"For as many as are led by the Spirit of God, they are the sons of God" (Rom. 8:14).

"God sent forth his Son . . . to redeem them that were under the law, that we might receive the adoption of sons" (Gal. 4:4,5).

"Having predestinated us unto the adoption of children by Jesus Christ to himself" (Eph. 1:5).

God has determined that everyone who will put his trust in His Son should be adopted into His family as sons. It is an amazing thing. We are the sons of One who is God, and we are and ever will be the objects of His love and His devotion.

The verse goes on to state our *future relationship.* "And it doth not yet appear what we shall be: but we know that, when he shall appear, we shall be like him; for we shall see him as he is" (I John 3:2).

God our Father is righteous. Our future experience will be that we will stand in His presence looking just like His precious Son, who is made unto us righteousness. I love the confidence of John. *We know.* How much do we know?

"I KNOW whom I have believed, and am persuaded that he is able to keep that which I have committed unto him against that day" (II Tim. 1:12).

"BEING CONFIDENT of this very thing, that he which hath begun a good work in you will perform it until the day of Jesus Christ" (Phil. 1:6).

"These things have I written unto you that believe on the name of the Son of God, that ye may KNOW that ye have eternal life, and that ye may believe on the name of the Son of God" (I John 5:13). The American Standard Version translates the last phrase, "even unto you that believe on the name of the Son of God."

Did you ever stop to think of it? When God gets through with you and with me, we are going to be just like His Son. What will we look like when we get to heaven? Just like Jesus. My, what a transformation! Only God could do this. We tend to look at the other fellow and say, "I am so glad he is going to be changed." Yes, but we are going to be changed, too. We can look at other Christians today and find plenty of ground to criticize. But let us not do that. Wait until God is through with all of us. God is not going to be satisfied with any of us until we stand in his presence like His Son. You will never be satisfied with me, and I will never be satisfied with you until we look just like Jesus. I say again, only God can do that. Isn't it wonderful that we have this joyful anticipation of the coming of our Saviour, whom having not seen we love?

"For now we see through a glass, darkly; but then face to face: now I know in part; but then shall I know even as also I am known" (I Cor. 13:12).

"For whom he did foreknow, he also did predestinate to be conformed to the image of his Son, that he might be the firstborn among many brethren" (Rom. 8:29).

"For our conversation is in heaven; from whence also we look for the Saviour, the Lord Jesus Christ: Who shall change our vile body, that it may be fashioned like unto his glorious body, according to the working whereby he is able even to subdue all things unto himself" (Phil. 3:20,21).

What a blessed hope! Today we can live in the anticipation of His coming.

We have noted that we are encouraged in our fellowship because of our present relationship as the sons of God. It is this relationship which causes the world not to know us, because it did not know Him. We are also encouraged by the future prospect that when the Lord Jesus comes, the dead in Christ will be raised, and we believers will be caught up together with them and will be transformed and glorified (I Thess. 4:13-18).

"And if Christ be in you, the body is dead because of sin; but the Spirit is life because of righteousness. But if the Spirit of him that raised up Jesus from the dead dwell in you, he that raised up Christ from the dead shall also quicken your mortal bodies by his Spirit that dwelleth in you" (Rom. 8:10,11).

"And if I go and prepare a place for you, I will come again, and receive you unto myself; that where I am, there ye may be also" (John 14:3).

"As for me, I will behold thy face in righteousness: I shall be satisfied, when I awake, with thy likeness" (Psa. 17:15).

Read also the passages in I Corinthians 15:51-57 and I Thessalonians 5:23,24.

We also read, "But we all, with open face beholding as in a glass the glory of the Lord, are changed into the same image from glory to glory, even as by the Spirit of the Lord" (II Cor. 3:18). If contemplation and occupation with

Christ affects our lives and changes our lives now, what will it be when we see Him face to face? *We shall be just like Him.*

May I add a solemn note here. When the world sees Him, it will be a time of judgment for them: "Behold, He cometh with clouds; and every eye shall see him, and they also which pierced him: and all kindreds of the earth shall wail because of him" (Rev. 1:7). The Christian looks forward with joyful anticipation, but the world shall wail.

You see, the first time He came to the world as a Saviour, but the next time He will return to the world as the Judge. "And the kings of the earth, and the great men, and the rich men, and the chief captains, and the mighty men, and every bondman, and every free man, hid themselves in the dens and in the rocks of the mountains; And said to the mountains and rocks, Fall on us, and hide us from the face of him that sitteth on the throne, and from the wrath of the Lamb" (Rev. 6:15,16). Twenty-seven times in the Book of Revelation He is called the Lamb of God. Men are going to be judged in the presence of the Lamb.

If you are unsaved, what is your hope? What is your prospect? When you leave this world, then what? It is an amazing thing that when we read the New Testament, we find that God has hope for the earth upon which we walk. It has the hope of being delivered from the curse of sin. The animal creation has hope (Rom. 8:18-25). The believer in Christ has hope. Did you ever stop to think of the one group which has no hope? There are no prospects ahead for those who are out of Christ, who have never received the Lord Jesus Christ as Saviour.

Life is only a fleeting shadow. We are here today and gone tomorrow. But you can have hope and you can have life. Take the Lord Jesus Christ, who died for you and rose again, as your own personal Saviour, and then you, too, will have hope. *In Him is Life.*

I do not remember where I read this but it is worth repeating:
"Sonship starts with life,
It is expressed in love,
It is marked by loyalty,
It culminates in likeness.
When we see Him, we shall be like Him!"

The following outline is by Dr. Griffith Thomas:
(The Apostle John, Eerdmans, pp. 279-283)

"WE ARE NOW HIS CHILDREN"

"The Fact of Sonship
  (I John 2:29 and 3:1)
The Mark of Sonship—practical righteousness
  (I John 2:29)
The Privilege of Sonship—objects of His love
  (I John 3:1)
The Consciousness of Sonship—we are His sons
  (I John 3:2)
The Mystery of Sonship—the world doesn't even know us
  (I John 3:1)
The Crown of Sonship—we shall be like Him
  (I John 3:2)
The Demands of Sonship—to purify ourselves as He
is pure
  (I John 3:3)"

Our present relationship and our hope for the future have a practical application in our *present experience.* "And every man that hath this hope in him purifieth himself, even as he is pure" (I John 3:3).

Every man that hath this hope in him has the incentive for holy living. The blessed hope and prospect of seeing Him face to face is a purifying hope. Notice that Christ Himself is the standard of Christian living. We are to purify ourselves even as He is pure. May I say that setting our hearts on Him always brings purification from defilement. When we shall see Him, we shall be like Him. What an incentive to live for God!

"Hencefore there is laid up for me a crown of righteousness, which the Lord, the righteous judge, shall give me at that day: and not to me only, but unto all them also that love his appearing" (II Tim. 4:8). Do you love His appearing? If you do, you will purify yourself even as He is pure. This is a sanctifying, a purifying hope. "See then that ye walk circumspectly, not as fools, but as wise, redeeming the time, because the days are evil" (Eph. 5:15,16).

THE OPPOSITION TO THE FELLOWSHIP

Whosoever committeth sin transgresseth also the law: for sin is the transgression of the law.

And ye know that he was manifested to take away our sins; and in him is no sin.

Whosoever abideth in him sinneth not: whosoever sinneth hath not seen him, neither known him.

Little children, let no man deceive you: he that doeth righteousness is righteous, even as he is righteous.

He that committeth sin is of the devil; for the devil sinneth from the beginning. For this purpose the Son of God was manifested, that he might destroy the works of the devil.

Whosoever is born of God doth not commit sin; for his seed remaineth in him; and he cannot sin, because he is born of God.

In this the children of God are manifest, and the children of the devil: whosoever doeth not righteousness is not of God, neither he that loveth not his brother.

For this is the message that ye heard from the beginning, that we should love one another.

> **Not as Cain, who was of that wicked one, and slew
> his brother. And wherefore slew he him? Because
> his own works were evil, and his brother's righteous.**
>
> **Marvel not, my brethren, if the world hate you
> (I John 3:4-13).**

It may come as a surprise to some to learn that there is
opposition to fellowship with God who is righteous. Before
we became Christians, we didn't have any opposition. The
devil was not opposed to us, the world was not opposed to
us, and the flesh was enjoying sin too much. When we
accepted the Saviour, we were translated out of the kingdom of darkness into the kingdom of God's Son. We
received the gift of eternal life and the indwelling of the
Spirit of God. Immediately we had three enemies: the
world, the flesh, and the devil.

As we study the opposition to the fellowship with God
who is righteous, we must first of all see what sin is. The
very first verse of this section defines it for us.

> **Whosoever committeth sin transgresseth also the
> law: for sin is the transgression of the law (I John
> 3:4).**

Sin is lawlessness. Sin is self-will and rebellion against the
person and law of God. It is not merely the transgression
of the law of the Ten Commandments or the law of the
Sermon on the Mount, but rather it is the spirit of
lawlessness. It is a life which is lived without respect or
consideration for the will and purpose of God.

I would like to say here that the law of Moses was not
given as a means of salvation but it was given to reveal
what sin is. I would like to list here eleven things which the
law does or does not do.

WHAT THE LAW CAN DO AND CANNOT DO

1. It makes sin exceeding sinful
   (Romans 7:7,13; 5:20).
2. It works wrath (Romans 4:15).
3. It is a ministration of death (II Cor. 3:7-9).
4. It is the strength of sin (I Cor. 15:56).
5. It brings a curse (Gal. 3:10).
6. It was added because of transgressions
   (Gal. 3:19).
7. By the law is the knowledge of sin (Romans
   3:20).
8. It is a schoolmaster to bring us to Christ (Gal.
   3:24).
9. The law is not of faith (Gal. 3:12).
10. The law cannot justify (Romans 3:20).
11. The law cannot give life (Gal. 3:21).

We see that the law is not of faith. It cannot give life. It cannot forgive or cleanse. It cannot make us strong. It demands, but gives no power to perform. The law makes sin exceeding sinful and gives a distinctive character to sin. It acts like a mirror to show us just how unclean we are (James 1:22-24). Mr. Moody used to say that we certainly do not wash our face with the mirror. The law shows us that we are transgressors, but it does not make us good. It cannot make us righteous; instead, it works wrath. The law served as a schoolmaster to bring us to Christ (Gal. 3:24). "Christ is the end of the law for righteousness to every one that believeth" (Rom. 10:4). "Sin shall not have dominion over you: for ye are not under the law, but under grace." (Rom. 6:14).

John has explained in this chapter that sin is the transgression of the law. It is lawlessness. Sin is contrary to the very character of a righteous God, and so sin breaks fellowship with God. Sin is an enemy and should have no place in the life of one who is a child of God.

The Apostle goes on to tell us that we have deliverance in our Lord Jesus Christ. The law is on one side of the cross, and the Christian is on the other side of the cross. This does not mean that Christians never sin. It does mean that the blood of Jesus Christ cleanses us from all sin, and that *He is our righteousness.*

And ye know that he was manifested to take away our sins; and in him is no sin (I John 3:5).

Two things are mentioned about our Lord in this verse. The one has to do with *His work,* and the other concerns *His Person.* We will consider the statement concerning His Person first.

"In Him is no sin." He is the absolutely sinless One with no trace of rebellion in Him. He is the exact opposite of what we are. In order to get a realistic look at ourselves, we must look at the Saviour. Jesus is God's perfect Man. Jesus, as He walked among men, lived the life that God wants men to live. Jesus could say to the religious leaders of His day, "Which of you convinceth Me of sin?" (John 8:46). He could tell the high priest that He had done nothing in secret. His life was an open book. I wonder, my friend, whether we would like others to see the secrets of our lives. Remember that Pilate had to acknowledge that he could find no fault in Him at all (John 18:38).

There are other Scriptures which refer to the truth that Jesus Christ is the sinless One.

"For he hath made him to be sin for us, WHO KNEW NO SIN; that we might be made the righteousness of God in him" (II Cor. 5:21).

"WHO DID NO SIN, neither was guile found in his mouth" (I Peter 2:22).

"For we have not an high priest which cannot be touched with the feeling of our infirmities; but was in all points tempted like as we are, YET WITHOUT SIN" (Heb. 4:15).

"WHICH OF YOU CONVINCETH ME OF SIN?" (John 8:46).

"IN HIM IS NO SIN" (I John 3:5).

His work, that which he has accomplished for us, is the basic, essential, blessed truth of the gospel. He had no sin in Himself, but He was manifested to take away our sins. The sinless One became sin. He was a fit sacrifice, and He put away our sin by the sacrifice of Himself. We should make no apology or allowance for sin when we realize that our Lord was manifested to take away our sins.

"Thou shalt call his name JESUS: for he shall save his people from their sins" (Matt. 1:21).

"Behold the Lamb of God, which taketh away the sin of the world" (John 1:29).

"Who gave himself for our sins, that he might deliver us from this present evil world" (Gal. 1:4).

"But now once in the end of the world hath he appeared to put away sin by the sacrifice of himself" (Heb. 9:26).

"But this man, after he had offered one sacrifice for sins forever, sat down on the right hand of God" (Heb. 10:12).

"All we like sheep have gone astray; we have turned every one to his own way; and the LORD hath laid on him the iniquity of us all" (Isa. 53:6).

In the eighth verse the Apostle goes on to tell us that He was manifested so that He might destroy the works of the devil.

> **For This purpose the Son of God was manifested, that he might destroy the works of the devil (I John 3:8b).**

I personally believe that the Lord Jesus Christ and the devil had a personal conflict. As a man, Christ faced the devil in person and defeated him. In His death, Christ triumphed over the devil. It is a wonderful truth that He guarantees to us deliverance from the power of the devil. There is one thing that is absolutely sure: the devil has no authority over those who are in Christ Jesus. Our Lord was manifested to take away our sins and to destroy the works of the devil.

"Forasmuch then as the children are partakers of flesh and blood, he also himself likewise took part of the same; that through death he might destroy him that had the power of death, that is, the devil; and deliver them who through fear of death were all their lifetime subject to bondage" (Heb. 2:14,15).

"Blotting out the handwriting of ordinances that was against us, which was contrary to us, and took it out of the way, nailing it to his cross; and having spoiled principalities and powers, he made a shew of them openly, triumphing over them in it" (Col. 2:14,15). "In it" means in the cross.

"Now is the judgment of this world: now shall the prince of this world be cast out" (John 12:31).

What a wonderful deliverance He has made for us! Not only has He delivered us from the power of sin and Satan, but He has made us His children. We cannot repeat too often what John is showing us in this Epistle. The great yearning of the heart of God is that His children will walk in fellowship with Him. The requirement for walking with God is that we must be righteous. He has made provision for this in Christ Jesus. So then, if I am a child of One who is righteous, righteousness should characterize my life. "And that ye put on the new man, which after God is created in righteousness and true holiness" (Eph. 4:24).

Now let us review the thrust of this third chapter. In the first three verses, the Apostle encourages us because we are in Christ, and we are His children, and it is because of this that we can have fellowship with Him. In the section from verse four to verse thirteen, he shows us the opposition to fellowship with God. That opposition is because of sin and so, in verse four, he shows us what sin is. It is lawlessness. However, there is a solution to the problem of sin, and this is stated in verses five and eight. The answer to our problem is that Christ was manifested to put away sin, and

He was manifested to destroy the works of the devil. Now, as a demonstration of what he is teaching us, he gives to us the contract between two families in the section from verse six to thirteen. Those two families are the children of God and the children of the devil. It is a contrast between righteousness and sin.

The man in Christ Jesus is declared righteous by God. The believer in Christ is looked upon by God as being righteous with that righteousness which is the mark of divine sonship. Therefore, righteousness will manifest this relationship to God and be the evidence of it. *Practical righteousness is a mark of divine sonship.*

This does not mean that a Christian will never sin. It does mean that the child of God does not *want* to sin. The believer in Christ does not habitually sin, so sinning is not the rule of his life. He is not dominated by sin. It is true that the Christian may fail God, but the pattern of his life is not one of rebellion and sinfulness against God. Rather, his desire is to please God.

Because this is true, the Christian may get disheartened when he does sin. Let me encourage you, my Christian friend, when you get disheartened about this. Have you stopped to think that the man of the world does not get disheartened over sin? The unsaved man lives in sin. He is full of sin, full of self-will, full of unrighteousness. His relationship is not to God but is to the enemy, the devil, and therefore sin characterizes and dominates his life. The devil was a liar and a murderer from the beginning, and so those who reject the Saviour and follow the devil will manifest this by lives of sin.

The believer who is born of God is a new creation. This is stated in II Corinthians 5:17. The manner of this new birth is explained in John 1:12,13. This new creation is created in righteousness and true holiness according to Ephesians 4:24. This new creation which is born of God does not commit sin. It is born of God and God is righteous.

> **Whosoever is born of God doth not commit sin; for his seed remaineth in him; and he cannot sin, because he is born of God (I John 3:9).**

This is restated later in this same Epistle. "We know that whosoever is born of God sinneth not; but he that is begotten of God keepeth himself, and that wicked one toucheth him not" (I John 5:18).

This new creation dwells in mortal, fleshly bodies, and so it is true that there are Christians who have been living somewhat in rebellion against God. This is a passing thing. If a person is really a child of God and is living in rebellion against God, then God will deal with him as with a son. "Whom the Lord loveth he chasteneth, and scourgeth every son whom he receiveth" (Heb. 12:6). Chastening is not a pleasant thing to experience (Heb. 12:11), but God uses it to keep His children from disobedience and to produce righteousness in character and in life.

God does not chasten those who are not His children. In fact, Hebrews 12:8 informs us that if we do not receive chastisement, the possibility is that we are not the children of God. I can remember that my mother did not chasten the neighbor's children, but she surely chastened us. So, whom the Lord loveth, He chasteneth.

If you really love the Lord, sin will not characterize your life. If you love to sin and love to rebel against the things of God, then you should examine your heart to find out if you are truly trusting the Saviour. A new creation, born of God, is created in righteousness and true holiness.

Now the Apostle John goes on to give us an illustration of these two families and the characteristics of the families.

> **For this is the message that ye heard from the beginning, that we should love one another.**
>
> **Not as Cain, who was of that wicked one, and slew his brother, And wherefore slew he him? Because his own works were evil, and his brother's righteous.**

Marvel not, my brethren, if the world hate you (I John 3:11-13).

Cain and Abel were the sons of Adam and Eve. Their story is told in Genesis 4. Both boys had been taught by their parents. They understood the fact of sin. They knew that One would come, the Seed of the woman, who would provide redemption. They knew that they must bring an offering as they came to worship God, and they knew the kind of offering they should bring and its significance.

Abel took a firstling of his flock, a lamb without blemish, to offer as a sacrifice. We read in Hebrews 11:4 "By faith Abel offered unto God a more excellent sacrifice than Cain." In the bringing of his sacrifice he acknowledged that he was a sinner and that he believed in the promise of a coming Redeemer.

Cain, on the other hand, brought the fruit of a cursed ground as his sacrifice. He ignored the fact of sin and also the promise of God concerning a Saviour. He was an unbeliever. The great difference was that Abel responded to God's revelation and submitted to His will. He brought his offering in faith and obedience. Cain was disobedient and willful, coming to God with that which God could not receive.

Men today still seek to bring to God the fruit of a sinful, fallen nature, but a holy, righteous God cannot accept that which is sinful. Yet God was longsuffering with Cain, pleading with him to bring a sin offering. He rebelled against God, then rose up against his brother and slew him. He was not angry at Abel. He was angry at God. He demonstrated that anger by slaying God's man.

John tells us in our text that Cain was of that wicked one and slew his brother. Why did he slay him? Because his own works were evil, and his brother's works were righteous. In other words, the heart of Cain in his attitude toward God manifested itself in his disobedience to the Word of God. The heart of Abel in his attitude toward God manifested itself in his obedience to the Word of God.

Let us make this very, very clear. One is not a child of the devil because he is bad nor is one a child of God because he is good. A child of God is a person who has accepted God's way of salvation in Christ Jesus. "As many as received him, to them gave he power to become the sons of God, even to them that believe on his name" (John 1:12). God has declared that He will save, He will forgive, He will give eternal life to those people who accept His salvation in Christ Jesus.

Cain knew how he should come and knew what he should bring. He rebelled against God because his heart was evil. It was because of this evil heart that his works were bad. On the other hand, Abel had accepted God's way of salvation, and his heart was right toward God. Therefore, he responded in simple obedience, and in his sacrifice he manifested his faith and his obedience. This is the reason he was accepted of God.

May I give a word of caution. All people on earth are divided into two families. One is either a child of God or a child of the devil. Christians, please be very slow ever to call anyone a child of the devil! It does say in Ephesians 2:3 that we were all by nature the children of wrath. However, when Scripture uses the term "children of the devil" as in John 8 and here in this Epistle, it refers to people who hate the Lord Jesus. In our Lord's day, He referred to the religious leaders who were spurning and rebelling against Him, the Son of God. Here in this Epistle, a child of the devil is illustrated by Cain, who had an evil heart and manifested it in his refusal to obey God or to accept God's way of sacrifice.

May I also give a word of encouragement. God desires an intimacy with us. God makes known His ways only to those who walk with Him. "He made known his ways unto Moses, his acts unto the children of Israel" (Psa. 103:7). Israel saw only His acts, His power. Moses was given to know God's ways. How wonderful it is to know that God wants to sit down with us, through the Word of God and the Holy Spirit, and teach us the things pertaining to Himself. He yearns to open His heart to us and show us the purposes that He has for the world. So let us be warm-hearted, in love with the Saviour. When we read the Word of God, let us let *Him* come into our lives.

THE EVIDENCE OF THE FELLOWSHIP

It is interesting that in chapter two we learned that love for the brethren is the evidence of fellowship with God who is light. Here we learn that love for the brethren is also the evidence of fellowship with God who is righteous.

> We know that we have passed from death unto life, because we love the brethren. He that loveth not his brother abideth in death.
>
> Whosoever hateth his brother is a murderer: and ye know that no murderer hath eternal life abiding in him.
>
> Hereby perceive we the love of God, because he laid down his life for us: and we ought to lay down our lives for the brethren.
>
> But whoso hath this world's good, and seeth his brother have need, and shutteth up his bowels of compassion from him, how dwelleth the love of God in him?
>
> My little children, let us not love in word, neither in tongue; but in deed and in truth (I John 3:14-18).

We know. This is experiential knowledge. How do I know when I am in fellowship with God who is righteous? How do I know that I am a child of God? We know that we have passed from death unto life because we love the brethren. He that loveth not his brother abideth in death. If I say that I am the child of God who is righteous, then I am going to manifest that by a righteous life, displayed in love for the brethren.

Remember, we do not receive eternal life by loving the brethren! Eternal life is a free gift from God received by faith (John 5:24; John 3:16; Rom. 6:23). Our faith has the risen Christ as its object. We have dared to believe that what God says is true. We have put our trust in the Saviour who died to put away our sins, and so we have received eternal life. This is what His Word declares. God sees our faith and counts it to us for righteousness. Men cannot see our faith, but men can experience our love! Then how can we know in our experience that we have eternal life? It will be manifested in our love for the brethren. *Life is not received by love. Life is received by relationship through faith. Love is the action of that life!*

The passage from verses 5-13 shows us that eternal life will be manifested in us by righteousness. If a believer is in fellowship with a God who is righteous, then his acts will be righteous.

> Little children, let no man deceive you: he that
> doeth righteousness is righteous, even as he is
> righteous (I John 3:7).

Now John is getting right down into our hearts and telling us that if we claim to be joined to God who is righteous, it will be evident by our love for the brethren. Loving the unsaved is not mentioned here; the evidence is loving the brethren. So the manifestation of our fellowship with God is a life of practical righteousness and a love for the brethren.

The next logical question would be: how are we to manifest our love for the brethren? John answers this by an illustration.

> Hereby perceive we the love of God, because he laid
> down his life for us: and we ought to lay down our
> lives for the brethren (I John 3:16).

He expresses the same thought in the fourth chapter. " In this was manifested the love of God toward us, because that God sent his only begotten Son into the world, that we might live through him. Herein is love, not that we love God, but that he loved us, and sent his Son to be the propitiation for our sins" (I John 4:9,10).

God manifested His love to us by sacrifice. *We manifest our love for the brethren by sacrifice.* We ought to lay down our lives for the brethren. He is not talking about martyrdom here. He is talking about loving our brother with the kind of love He manifested. This is one of the greatest needs among God's people today. "A new commandment I give unto you, That ye love one another; as I have loved you, that ye also love one another. By this shall all men know that ye are my disciples, if ye have love one to another" (John 13:34,35).

How shall we love each other? Even as He has loved us! This is a love that must come from God. "The love of God is shed abroad in our hearts by the Holy Ghost which is given unto us" (Rom. 5:5). It is not our doctrine, nor our ability, nor some special gift of the Spirit, but it is love of the brethren that is the evidence of fellowship with God who is righteous. The Lord wants this love of the brethren to be a reality, not just empty profession. He wants deeds, not just talk. *God sees my faith but men should experience my love. Christianity is love in action.*

Let us not judge other Christians in the light of our own conscience or in the light of our experience. It is so easy to judge the falling brother and to criticize those who do not walk the way we think they should walk. Remember, there are those in the family of God who are mature Christians, and there are those who are not mature. We do not expect a baby to live and act like a grown man or woman. Likewise, there must be time for growth in the things of God. Immature Christians, new Christians, babes in Christ may say things and do things that are not right, yet they belong to the Saviour. We are to love them. If God loves them, we ought to, too. "Brethren, if a man be overtaken in a fault, ye which are spiritual, restore such an one in the spirit of meekness; considering thyself, lest thou also be tempted" (Gal. 6:1).

Satan has knitted together all the antichristian forces, and he also succeeds in separating the believers from within. Love is the need among professing Christians today. We who love the Saviour and who love the Word of God should be genuine in our love one for the other. We are to love those who love the Saviour. This does not mean that we are to compromise our own faith in the Saviour or our conviction of truth. It does mean we are to love anyone who belongs to the Saviour. How are we ever going to come together in a oneness of doctrine and of life unless we first love one another in Christ?

What a testimony it would be before the world if we loved even those who don't agree with us on every point! Personally, I will go a long way with a person who really is genuine in his love for the Lord Jesus Christ. We must keep in mind that all Christians do not have the same opportunities, they are not equally taught, they do not equally love the Word of God. Yet the command is that all Christians should love one another. The tragedy is that some Christians will even go to the world to criticize another Christian. This is what the world loves. It is like a sweet morsel under their tongue. It gives them ammunition against the gospel. My brother, if we must criticize another Christian, let us do it in love and to his face, or, if necessary, before the people of God. Let us never go to the world and there run down the people of God. We preach Christ. Then let us also manifest the love of Christ!

THE RESULT OF THE FELLOWSHIP

The result of our fellowship with God who is righteous is that we have confidence and assurance.

1. We have assurance in fellowship.

And hereby we know that we are of the truth, and shall assure our hearts before him.

For if our heart condemn us, God is greater than our heart, and knoweth all things.

Beloved, if our heart condemn us not, then have we confidence toward God (I John 3:19-21).

I am thankful for that word "know," which shows there is no doubting or questioning. This is not talking about assurance of salvation. This verse is speaking about assurance of the fact that we are in fellowship with God so that we have a boldness before God based on a walk with the righteous God.

"If our heart condemn us . . . " When we come before God, our heart is going to be convicted if there is failure or any disobedience to His Word. God is greater than our heart. If we know what we have done, certainly God knows what we have done. If we come into the presence of God and feel condemned, it is because we are out of fellowship and are walking apart from Him. We cannot hide anything from Him. He knows all things. He longs for our heart to respond to His heart. We are to confess our sin to Him as we learned in I John 1:9. He has promised to forgive us and to cleanse us from all unrighteousness.

"If our heart condemn us not . . . " If there is nothing between our heart and God's heart, then we have boldness and confidence before God. This is not a demanding spirit but an attitude of worship and of humility. We come as the children of God but still His creatures. There is a reverence and awe and worship in fellowship with God. There is also a peace and a confidence before God. The best way to describe it is to give an illustration from the Scripture.

In the book of Exodus, chapters 32 and 33, we are told something of the relationship between God and Moses. God had brought the people of Israel out of Egypt under the leadership of Moses. They had been brought through the Red Sea, miraculously fed, given water in the wilderness by

God. Then Moses went up on the mountain to receive the Lord's law. Meanwhile, Aaron and the people made a molten calf and worshiped it. God was displeased and told Moses that He would blot out this idolatrous nation and make a great nation of Moses. Moses said to God, "You cannot do that. Then your promises to Abraham, Isaac, and Jacob would not avail. Furthermore, what would the Egyptians say? You would be dishonored among the nations of the earth." Notice the boldness of Moses. He pleaded with God on the basis of God's promises and the glory of His Person. And the Lord heard the prayer of Moses. Then the Lord promised Moses, "My presence shall be with thee, and I will give thee rest" (Ex. 33:14). Again, notice the boldness and the confidence of Moses as he asks God to show him His glory. Fellowship with the eternal God brings such confidence.

Oh, that we might come before God with such openness of heart! If you have failed God, remember He has made the provision for you to be forgiven and cleansed. If your heart condemns you in His presence, why don't you confess your sin and be cleansed from all unrighteousness? Then you can go on to enjoy the day in fellowship with God.

2. Another result of fellowship with God who is righteous is assurance in prayer.

> **And whatsoever we ask, we receive of him, because we keep his commandments, and do those things that are pleasing in his sight (I John 3:22).**

When we are walking in fellowship with God, all doubts are removed and we will come to Him in prayer. Communion with God excludes all false petitions. We will not want that which is outside the will of God but will seek to please Him. Whatsoever we ask of Him we will receive because we are obedient to His Word and because we trust

Him. What are His commandments to us? The next verse tells us.

> And this is his commandment, That we should believe on the name of his Son Jesus Christ, and love one another, as he gave us commandment (I John 3:23).

Let us look ahead in this same Epistle to another expression of this same confidence in prayer. "And this is the confidence that we have in him, that, if we ask any thing according to his will, he heareth us: And if we know that he hear us, whatsoever we ask, we know that we have the petitions that we desired of him" (I John 5:14,15).

People often say to me, "I stood on these prayer promises and God didn't answer me." May I ask some questions? What did you ask for? Did you ask according to His will (I John 5:14)? Did you ask those things that are pleasing in His sight (I John 3:22)? Were you asking for your own selfish purposes or for His honor and praise and glory? Let us consider the Scriptures that give us the ground for answered requests.

"And in that day ye shall ask me nothing. Verily, verily, I say unto you, Whatsoever ye shall ask the Father in my name, he will give it you. Hitherto have ye asked nothing in my name: ask, and ye shall receive, that your joy may be full. These things have I spoken unto you in proverbs: but the time cometh, when I shall no more speak unto you in proverbs, but I shall shew you plainly of the Father. At that day ye shall ask in my name: and I say not unto you, that I will pray the Father for you: For the Father himself loveth you, because ye have loved me, and have believed that I came out from God. I came forth from the Father, and am come into the world: again, I leave the world, and go to the Father" (John 16:23-28).

Jesus is saying, "In that day," that is, in the day when the Spirit of God indwells you, "you shall ask me nothing." Why is this? It is because in that day "you shall ask the Father in My name." Jesus mentions the Father six

times in six verses. Our Lord is emphasizing this. It is
because of relationship to the Father that our Lord is not
going to make our requests for us. *The Father Himself
loves us.* We can come into the presence of the Father in
all the righteousness and beauty of our Saviour, and thus
we may come with confidence. If there is nothing between
us and the Father, then Jesus says, "Whatsoever you shall
ask the Father in My name, he will give it you."

I am going to be bold enough to state that if we come
to the Father under these conditions, we will invariably
pray in the will of God. I believe this is what it means in
Jude 20, "Praying in the Holy Ghost." We can have a
confidence, a rest, an assurance in the presence of God so
that we are not afraid to make our requests because He
loves us. Did you mark this? Not because we love Him but
because He loves us! "For the Father himself loveth you."
When we make our request, there must be nothing between
us and the Father, nothing for our heart to condemn.

Jesus sets forth another condition for answered prayer.
"Whatsoever ye shall ask in my name, that will I do, that
the Father may be glorified in the Son. If ye shall ask any
thing in my name, I will do it" (John 14:13,14).

Here is another sure promise, but it does require our
obedience. Do we make our requests so that the Father will
be glorified in the Son? The Lord is telling us that we have
this tremendous resource of coming into the presence of
God in order that we might manifest to the world the
character, the heart, the love, and the compassion of God.
An exegesis of this chapter would point out that Jesus is
answering the request, "Show us the Father." Jesus tells of
the resources that we have, and one of these is prayer.
When we, as Christians, walk in fellowship with God, then
by the Spirit of God we get to know His will. Then our
will and our wish will be that the Father might be glorified
in Jesus Christ in the midst of men.

Let us consider another condition. "If ye abide in me,
and my words abide in you, ye shall ask what ye will, and

it shall be done unto you" (John 15:7). Are we abiding in Him? Is His Word abiding in us? *Then,* we ask what we will. Well, then what will our desire be? What would we pray? We will pray His will! He will put His desire into our hearts. Then, as we pray in the Spirit of God, He answers that prayer. Invariably! Because it is prayed through the Spirit of God in an obedient heart! As we walk in fellowship with the Saviour, by the Spirit of God we come to know the desires of God's heart. Then, in cooperation with Him, we use prayer, that tool, that channel, that weapon which God has given us. We become instruments in the hands of God for the performance of His will and the carrying out of his purpose for the glorifying of His Son among men.

The Christian has two great weapons from God. One is the Word of God, which is the sword of the Spirit. It is by the Word of God that people are brought to Christ. It is by the Word of God that the Christians are cleansed. The other weapon is prayer. Prayer is the instrument by which we touch the sovereign, omnipotent God who has all authority in heaven and in earth.

We Christians have a tremendous responsibility to pray for our country and government and all in authority. We should pray that the church of Christ may realize its position and place, carrying to the world the wonderful story of redeeming grace. We should pray for the world. We cannot read the Bible without realizing that prayer is the weapon which God has put into the hands of His children. Abraham pleaded for Sodom and Gomorrah and for Abimelech and his nation. Moses pleaded for Israel. Job prayed for his friends. Ezra, Daniel, Jeremiah prayed for their people.

We need to know these truths concerning prayer so that we do not become discouraged and disheartened in our praying. The Lord loves us with an everlasting love. Nothing delights Him more than that His children come to Him with their requests, with their worship, and with their praises. We come in humility before a loving, eternal, sovereign God, knowing that He is able to work out His own purposes. We can touch the throne of God. What a privilege is ours.

3. The third result of fellowship with God who is righteous is that we have assurance because of our union with Him.

We have been looking at the requirements for effectual prayer and found the two specific commandments in verse 23. We should believe on the name of His Son, Jesus Christ, and we should love one another. This, then, leads to the ground for our confidence, which is our union with Him.

> **And he that keepeth his commandments dwelleth in him, and he in him. And hereby we know that he abideth in us, by the Spirit which he hath given us (I John 3:24).**

Here is the fact of our amazing union with Christ. Our Lord said the same thing in John 14. "And I will pray the Father, and he shall give you another Comforter, that he may abide with you for ever; Even the Spirit of truth; whom the world cannot receive, because it seeth him not, neither knoweth him: but ye know him; for he dwelleth with you, and shall be in you. I will not leave you comfortless: I will come to you. Yet a little while, and the world seeth me no more; but ye see me: because I live, ye shall live also. At that day ye shall know that I am in my Father, and ye in me, and I in you" (John 14:16-20).

"At that day" again refers to the day when the Spirit of God will indwell you. Because He is abiding in us by His Spirit, we have this wonderful union between the Saviour and His people, and this gives us confidence to come into the presence of God.

Many of God's people who love the Saviour really know so little about our bond with Him. The same union that Jesus has with the Father is the union that Jesus has with us. What confidence! What assurance! What joy! We are eternally, completely, absolutely joined to the Son of God. There is no power on earth or in hell that can break that relationship and that union. If this would ever grip our hearts as it should, we would be an entirely different people.

I John 2:28 has this same thought of standing before Him with confidence and not being ashamed before Him at His coming. This is what God wants of you and of me. Because of our union with Jesus, we can have this confidence, this assurance, this boldness. Our Lord told us in John 4:23 that the Father is seeking worshipers.

The first thing that He wants from His people is worship. That is why the Saviour asked Peter three times in John 21, "Peter, do you love Me?" He didn't ask Peter whether he would serve Him, or do this thing or that thing. The all-important question is whether we *love Him*. Everything else will come as an outflow of a love for the Saviour.

We need to get back to basic, foundational truth. We have confidence not only because our sins have been put away, not only because we can come into His presence as His children, not only because we stand before God in all the beauty and righteousness of Christ, but also because of our union with our Saviour. His life has become our life. His desire has become our desire. His will has become our will. His purpose has become our purpose. We are going to cooperate with Him whatever *He* wants. This is Christianity in action. This is our love for *Him* in action.

Some people become so occupied with an experience they have had that they shut out the presence of the Saviour. They talk about experience but are ignorant of the Word of God and of this wonderful union with the Saviour. That is a life on the level of shallow emotionalism. It is true that God has given us emotions, but let us not live in emotionalism. Let us get down to the very heart of God, to the reality of our union with the Saviour. Let us stop playing at being religious, and let us walk with God and become available to Him. Then He will find us channels through whom He can display Himself to the hearts and lives of men and women on the earth.

Now let us take a quick overview of this chapter.

In the first three verses, we had the encouragement to have fellowship with God who is righteous. There is a present encouragement because we are now His children. There is a future encouragement, for His purpose will be completed and we shall all be conformed to the image of His Son. Everyone who has this hope in him purifieth himself even as He is pure.

The opposition to the fellowship was set forth in verses 4-13. We are exhorted not to marvel if we are hated by the world. The world had no place for Christ and never understood Him. The world could only cast Him out. So we are not to be surprised when we follow the Lord Jesus to find that this same old world will not want us either.

The evidence of fellowship with God who is righteous is love for the brethren, verses 14-18. God calls us to reality. We are not to love only in word but also in deed.

Verses 19-24 show us the assurance in fellowship because God has made provision to remove the barrier that has broken fellowship. We can have assurance in prayer, confidence to come to the throne of grace and know that He is going to meet our needs because the Father loves us and because we are in a union with Jesus Christ. There is no power on earth or hell that can break that union with Him because the Spirit of God indwells us.

May the Lord make these wonderful truths very precious to your hearts. May you know something of the wonder of fellowship and union with the Son of God.

THE TEST OF THE FELLOWSHIP

Beloved believe not every spirit, but try the spirits whether they are of God: because many false prophets are gone out into the world.

Hereby know ye the Spirit of God: Every spirit that confesseth that Jesus Christ is come in the flesh is of God:

And every spirit that confesseth not that Jesus Christ is come in the flesh is not of God: and this is that spirit of antichrist, whereof ye have heard that it should come; and even now already is it in the world.

Ye are of God, little children, and have overcome them: because greater is he that is in you, than he that is in the world.

They are of the world: therefore speak they of the world, and the world heareth them.

We are of God: he that knoweth God heareth us; he that is not of God heareth not us. Hereby know we the spirit of truth, and the spirit of error. (I John 4:1-6).

God asks us to test people. We are to use spiritual discernment because many false prophets are gone out into the world. How can we do this? One man says the Bible teaches this, and another man says the Bible teaches that. Someone else says the Bible is not to be trusted at all. How can we know that which is of God and that which is not of God?

We are to test a person on the basis of what he confesses about the *Person of Jesus Christ.*

Hereby know ye the Spirit of God: Every spirit that confesseth that Jesus Christ is come in the flesh is of God:

> **And every spirit that confesseth not that Jesus Christ is come in the flesh is not of God: and this is that spirit of antichrist, whereof ye have heard that it should come; and even now already is it in the world (I John 4:2,3).**

When John wrote this Epistle, he was facing what is known as Gnosticism. The Gnostics were those who believed that Jesus Christ was an emanation from God, a created being. They considered Him to be higher than the angels but not truly God, not God manifest in the flesh. Their ground for this was that they believed the flesh to be evil. Of course, we can agree with that. The desires of our flesh are evil and get us into trouble. So they asked how a holy God could be made manifest in that which is evil.

John faces this question. Who are those who are true? Who are those who really believe the Word of God? "Every spirit that confesseth that Jesus Christ is come in the flesh is of God." Permit me to change the wording. Everyone who confesses that Jesus Christ is God Incarnate is of God.

Both John and Peter declared that Jesus Christ is God manifest in the flesh. "And the Word was made flesh, and dwelt among us, (and we beheld his glory, the glory as of the only begotten of the Father,) full of grace and truth" (John 1:14).

Later, on the Isle of Patmos, John saw Jesus in His glory. "And when I saw him, I fell at his feet as dead. And he laid his right hand upon me, saying unto me, Fear not; I am the first and the last: I am he that liveth, and was dead; and, behold, I am alive for evermore, Amen; and have the keys of hell and of death" (Rev. 1:17,18).

Peter writes, "For we have not followed cunningly devised fables, when we made known unto you the power and coming of our Lord Jesus Christ, but were eyewitnesses of his majesty" (II Pet. 1:16).

Do not try to say that Jesus Christ did not make that same claim! In the fifth chapter of John the Jews said to

Him in effect, "Who do You think You are? God?" And they sought to kill Him. He answered them, "Yes! My Father has the authority to raise the dead and make them alive. That is exactly what I can do!" We read at the end of John chapter 8 that when Jesus said to the Jews of His day, "Your father Abraham rejoiced to see my day: and he saw it, and was glad," the Jews knew exactly what He was talking about. Then said the Jews unto him, "Thou art not yet fifty years old, and hast thou seen Abraham?" His answer to them was, "Verily, verily, I say unto you, Before Abraham was, I am." *I am! Jehovah!* I am the eternal God. So the Jews tried to kill Him.

That person who denies that Jesus Christ is God manifest in the flesh is not of God. I say very bluntly that a great many ecclesiastical leaders in our country are not Christian because they deny the Incarnate Word of God. Let me say that if Jesus Christ is not God Incarnate, if He is not the sinless Son of God, then we do not have a Saviour. Then He had to die for His own sin and could not have died to put away sin by the sacrifice of Himself. This is precisely what these people are saying. They teach that when He died on the cross, He died as a martyr. They take the very words of Scripture and twist them to deceive the people of God. Remember that in II Corinthians 11:13,14 we are told that Satan himself is transformed into an angel of light, and that *his* ministers will come as ministers of righteousness. The Word of God declares that we are to try the spirits to see if they are of God.

In chapter three we studied the contrast between two families, the children of God and the children of the devil. Here we find a contrast between two spirits, the spirit of Christ and the spirit of antichrist. "Every spirit that confesseth that Jesus Christ is come in the flesh is of God."

The contrast to this is the spirit of antichrist. We have already learned that this exists (I John 2:18). Now it is defined as the denial that Jesus Christ is the Incarnate Word of God. So we find that we can test the *character* of those who claim to speak for God on the basis of what they teach and believe about the person of Jesus Christ.

May I remind you again that Satan will come as an angel of light and that Satan's ministers come as the ministers of righteousness for the purpose of deceiving the people of God. There is abundant evidence of this in the Scriptures. There is an abundance of counterfeiting of truth everywhere. Our Lord in Matthew 13:24-30 speaks the parable of the wheat and the tares. They both grow together until the harvest. In Exodus we find Moses, the servant of God, performing miracles, and immediately Jannes and Jambres (II Tim. 3:8), who were the magicians of Pharaoh, tried to imitate the things that Moses did. In Acts 8 Simon the sorcerer wanted to imitate Philip and Peter. In Acts 13 Paul is opposed by Elymas, the sorcerer.

Listen to the Apostle Peter. "But there were false prophets also among the people, even as there shall be false teachers among you, who privily shall bring in damnable heresies, even denying the Lord that bought them and bring upon themselves swift destruction . . . These are wells without water, clouds that are carried with a tempest; to whom the mist of darkness is reserved for ever" (II Peter 2:1 and 17). Then in II Peter 3:3-5 he goes on to point out that they are willingly ignorant. They do not want to know the truth. Mark these things!

Our Saviour gave His disciples a stern warning: "Many will say to me in that day, Lord, Lord, have we not prophesied in thy name? . . . then will I profess unto them, I never knew you" (Matt. 7:21-23). There are people who profess to be preachers, who profess to perform miracles in the name of Christ, and yet our Saviour will say, "I *never* knew you."

John is making it very, very clear to us. You see, one can *profess* knowledge of a fact and not accept it. We read, "Every spirit that confesseth that Jesus Christ is come in the flesh is of God." *Confesses!* This is a relationship by faith with the person of Jesus Christ.

The issue is always Christ. Is He God who took His place in the human family? "The Word was with God," and "the Word was God," and "the Word was made flesh" (John 1:1-3, 14). Jesus Christ is the image of the invisible God. In Him all the fulness of God is revealed. By Him all things consist (Col. 1:15-19). The fulness of the Godhead dwells in Him bodily (Col 2:9). He is the brightness of God's glory and the express image of His person (Heb. 1:3). The great question is the position that is given to Christ. Is *HE* the center of all? Is this Jesus of Nazareth confessed to be God manifest in the flesh, both Lord and Christ (Acts 2:22 and 36)? This is the issue.

Preachers may have enthusiasm and showmanship, but if they say that Jesus is just a prophet, a teacher, an ideal, and deny His person and His deity, then they have the spirit of antichrist. When we see religious leaders hating the Word of God and rebelling against the person of Christ, we know they have imbibed the spirit of antichrist. When leaders who deny the person of Christ advocate immorality and corruption, lawlessness and rebellion, then we are seeing the world preparing for the coming of the man of sin, the antichrist. He will be the personification of Satan. Just as our Saviour is God who was manifest in the flesh, so the antichrist will be the devil incarnate. He is going to gather the nations together and make war against the Saviour (Rev. 13 and 20). Satan and all his disciples hate God, hate the Son of God, hate the people of God, hate the Word of God. Let us not be deluded. The issue is very clear. If we stand for the Saviour, it is going to cost us something.

Since we are to take our place and stand for the Person of Christ against the world around us, there is a word of encouragement for us.

> **Ye are of God, little children, and have overcome them: because greater is he that is in you, than he that is in the world (I John 4:4).**

Our Lord has already conquered the powers of darkness. The victory is already assured. The Spirit of God who indwells you is greater than the prince of this world, the god of this age.

I want to tell you very frankly and joyfully that when one accepts the Saviour he has a relationship with the Saviour, and the Spirit of God indwells him. Greater is He, the Spirit of God, that is in you than he that is in the world. The Spirit of God is greater than any other force in the world or in hell, and so the victory is guaranteed.

I Corinthians 6:15 gives us this same assurance. If we love the Saviour, our bodies become members of Christ, and verse 19 states that we become the sanctuary of God, the temple of the Holy Spirit who is in us. It is the presence of this indwelling Spirit of God which guarantees the victory.

I love the testimony of a man who had been a slave to drink, a down-and-out alcoholic. He accepted the Lord Jesus Christ as Saviour and one day someone said to him, "So, you have the mastery over the devil at last." "No!" he said, "No, but I have in me the Master who has conquered the devil."

Of our own strength we cannot overcome sin, or the devil, or the world. But there is in the one who accepts the Saviour the Spirit of God, and "greater is He that is in you, than he that is in the world." You are of God, little children, and *have overcome* them.

We have been dealing with the fact that we are to test the spirits by testing their character. We test those who claim to speak for God on the basis of their belief about the person of Jesus Christ. Now we learn that we are also to test them on the basis of their *witness.* We are to determine the source of their witness and the effect of their witness.

They are of the world: therefore speak they of the world, and the world heareth them.

We are of God: he that knoweth God heareth us; he that is not of God heareth not us. Hereby know we the spirit of truth, and the spirit of error (I John 4:5,6).

We are to test not only the messenger but also the message. Those who have the spirit of antichrist, those who deny the Incarnate Word of God, are of the world. And the effect of their witness is that the world hears them. When we hear someone preach or teach, we need to discern whether the source of their teaching is of the world. Is it of Satan, the prince and god of this world? We can determine this because the world loves its own. The world speaks of its own. The world exalts man instead of exalting Christ. For the world, man is the center of attraction. We find in the world a rebellion against God because man wants to be the center. So people of the world are confused. Satan sees to it that they are confused. And I would say to you, until they have their faith and their love centered in the Saviour, they will continue to be confused.

People who are not of God belong to the world. They are of the world. They will gladly hear the world. They do not want to hear the things of God. In contrast, the believer loves to hear the message from God.

Therefore, we have a criterion by which we may test any witness that we hear. *The message of the world will make man the center. The message from the Spirit of God will always make Christ the center.*

"Howbeit when he, the Spirit of truth, is come, he will guide you into all truth: for he shall not speak of himself; but whatsoever he shall hear, that shall he speak: and he will show you things to come. He shall glorify me: for he shall receive of mine and shall shew it unto you" (John 16:13,14).

"Now then we are ambassadors for Christ, as though God did beseech you by us: we pray you in Christ's stead, be ye reconciled to God" (II Cor. 5:20).

"For we are labourers together with God: ye are God's husbandry, ye are God's building" (I Cor. 3:9).

Jesus, speaking of Himself and His work, told his disciples, "And ye are witnesses of these things" (Luke 24:48).

May I add here that the Word of God is the standard of truth. When you choose a church, be sure it is one where the worship of Christ is the central attraction and where you will be taught the Word of God. It is His Word that must be the rule and guide.

"I will worship toward thy holy temple, and praise thy name for thy lovingkindness and for thy truth: for thou hast magnified thy word above all thy name" (Psa. 138:2). In the revised text this is translated, "Thou has underwritten every word by Thy name."

"All scripture is given by inspiration of God, and is profitable for doctrine for reproof, for correction, for instruction in righteousness: That the man of God may be perfect, throughly furnished unto all good works" (II Tim. 3:16,17).

"These (the Bereans) were more noble than those in Thessalonica, in that they received the word with all readiness of mind, and searched the scriptures daily, whether those things were so" (Acts 17:11).

"Prove all things; hold fast that which is good" (I Thess. 5:21).

FELLOWSHIP
WITH GOD
WHO IS LOVE

The reason why so many people despise the God of love and have so little appreciation of the God of love is that they have never seen that God is righteous. The more we see the holy character of God, the more we will appreciate His love. There could be no display of His love without first of all a display of His righteous character. The gospel message does not reveal that God is love apart from the truth that God is righteous.

"For I am not ashamed of the gospel of Christ: for it is the power of God unto salvation to every one that believeth; to the Jew first, and also to the Greek. For therein is the RIGHTEOUSNESS OF GOD revealed from faith to faith: as it is written, The just shall live by faith" (Rom. 1:16,17).

"This then is the message which we have heard of him, and declare unto you, that GOD IS LIGHT" (I John 1:5).

"For our GOD IS A CONSUMING FIRE" (Heb. 12:29).

God must deal with sin in judgment, in righteousness, and in holiness. The only reason we can come into the presence of a holy God is because *His righteous character has been vindicated by His Son at the cross.* This is guaranteed to us by the resurrection. Because of this, we can enjoy fellowship with God who is holy, who is righteous, and who is love.

DIVINE LOVE MANIFESTED

Beloved, let us love one another: for love is of God; and every one that loveth is born of God, and knoweth God.

He that loveth not knoweth not God; for God is love.

In this was manifested the love of God toward us, because that God sent his only begotten Son into the world, that we might live through him.

Herein is love, not that we loved God, but that he loved us, and sent his Son to be the propitiation for our sins (I John 4:7-10).

We notice John's declaration of the fact that God is love. Our generation is very confused about the difference between love and lust. Many people think that immorality and moral corruption are not bad so long as people "love" each other. Some ecclesiastical leaders teach situation ethics. Isn't it really situation immorality?

We need to read I Corinthians 13 to learn what love is and to find how God describes love. Love suffereth long and is still kind. Love envieth not. Love is never puffed up, never behaveth itself unseemly. Love never seeks its own. Love is not easily provoked. Love thinketh no evil. Love believeth all things, hopeth all things. Love never fails. God is love!

God's love never fails. "Can a woman forget her sucking child, that she should not have compassion on the son of her womb? yea, they may forget, yet will I not forget thee" (Isa. 49:15).

If we love the Saviour, He will never leave us. Whatever we may be, His love is never affected by our frailty or weaknesses or failures. He loves us with an everlasting love. "Having loved his own which were in the world, he loved them unto the end" (John 13:1).

If the truth that every real believer in the Saviour is the object of His love and of His affection would really get hold of our hearts, then we would begin to love His people. Love responds to love. "A new commandment I give unto you, That ye love one another; as I have loved you, that ye also love one another. By this shall all men know that ye are my disciples, if ye have love one to another" (John 13:34,35). "This is my commandment, That ye love one another, as I have loved you" (John 15:12).

It is divine love that has been shed abroad in our hearts according to Romans 5:5: "The love of God is shed abroad in our hearts by the Holy Ghost which is given unto us." In other words, there *has been imparted to us divine love as well as divine life.*

May I plead with your heart, let us love one another. There are hundreds of Christians who are lonely, longing for a little manifestation of love from other Christians. They might not be very loveable, but perhaps this is because they need love. I know it is easy for us to love somebody who loves us, but God loves us even when we are unlovely and unloveable. "Herein is love, not that we loved God, but that he loved us" (I John 4:10). The very energy of God's nature to man is love.

Next, John shows to us the manifestation of that love.

> **In this was manifested the love of God toward us, because that God sent his only begotten Son into the world, that we might live through him.**
>
> **Herein is love, not that we loved God, but that he loved us, and sent his Son to be the propitiation for our sins (I John 4:9,10).**

People come to me and say, "Mr. Mitchell, I am not a pagan. I believe in God. I have my God and you have yours." Then I ask them, "What kind of a God do you have?" They will say that their God is a God of love. Then I ask them, "How do you know that your God is love?"

You see, my friend, apart from the Scriptures, apart from the revelation of God in Jesus Christ, there is no revelation that God is love. We do not find love in nature. One animal preys on another, and one fish feeds on another fish. No, we do not find love displayed in nature. There it is the survival of the fittest.

The great manifestation of the love of God was when He sent His only begotten Son into the world for us. If we reject Jesus Christ as God manifest in the flesh, if we say that Jesus Christ is not the Incarnate Word of God, then we have no basis to declare that God is love. God has manifested His love in Christ Jesus.

Love must have an object upon which to display itself. *We are the object of God's love.* It is an active love, and it is manifested by sacrifice. It is divine love. It is love which God extended to us even when we were unlovely and unloveable.

"But God commendeth his love toward us, in that, while we were yet sinners, Christ died for us" (Rom. 5:8).

"For if, when we were enemies, we were reconciled to God by the death of his Son, much more, being reconciled, we shall be saved by his life" (Rom. 5:10).

"Herein is love, not that we loved God, but that he loved us, and sent his Son to be the propitiation for our sins" (I John 4:10).

May I suggest this to your thinking? We manifest our love for God by our obedience to His Word. We found that in chapter two. In chapter three we learned that we manifest our love for each other by sacrifice. We do that through an imparted, divine love.

Here we find that God manifested or displayed His love for us by sending His only begotten Son into the world to die for us. Has it penetrated your heart that God loved you enough to send His Son to die for you? Do you know that God sent Jesus, heaven's Best, to die on the cross to put away your sins by the sacrifice of Himself, and then God raised Him from the dead and put Him at His own right hand and gave Him glory so that *your* faith might be in God (I Pet. 1:18-21)?

The purpose of this sacrifice made by God was that we might live. "Because that God sent His only begotten Son into the world, that we might live through Him" (I John 4:9b). God sent His Son on a mission. That mission was to take men who were *dead* in trespasses and sins and to transform them into children of God who should *live* with him eternally. I know of no message on God's earth that has such hope and love and joy and peace and satisfaction for the human heart. All that we need to do is to accept this divine gift which God has given to us and is now offering to us. "For the wages of sin is death; but the gift of God is eternal life through Jesus Christ our Lord" (Rom. 6:23).

Allow me to stop here for a moment and spend some time on these two verses in the Epistle of John since they are the very heart of the gospel. It is so frequently found that people think of the love of God and forget His righteousness and His holiness. These verses tell us how God can still be righteous and yet manifest His love to us, men and women who are unrighteous and have sinned. God cannot save people at the expense of His righteousness. Then He would no longer be righteous. There must be a putting away of sin and a satisfaction of the divine righteousness before God could ever save a single sinner. What righteousness could not do, love has done. *Love has provided the sacrifice.* Love has provided a Saviour. The Saviour satisfies (propitiates) the righteous character of God and the demands of His righteous law. This makes it possible for us to experience His love. Before God could ever open up His heart and open up His arms to receive men and women in their sins, His character had to be satisfied. His righteousness had to be vindicated. This is what our Saviour accomplished at the cross. I am persuaded that there is so little appreciation for the love of God today because men have never seen the God who is absolute in righteousness and holiness.

In order to emphasize the fact that the Son of God was sent on a mission, I want to call your attention to another study. John is the only one who calls Jesus "the only begotten Son of God." Five times in the New Testament, and only in John's writing, do we find this name. He is emphasizing that this is the One who is God, manifest in the flesh, the only begotten Son of God. We find it in John 1:14; John 1:18; John 3:16; John 3:18 and I John 4:9. Incidentally, John is also the only one who calls Him the "Lamb of God." We find that in John 1:29, John 1:36, and 27 times in the book of Revelation. Men will be judged in the presence of the Lamb of God.

Isaiah also emphasizes the fact that the Son of God was sent on a mission. "For unto us a child is born, unto us a son is given" (Isa. 9:6). Notice that the child was born, a real man coming through a human mother. But the Son was given. He was sent.

John, in his Gospel, emphasizes that the only begotten Son was never born. He was sent. Approximately 40 times in that Gospel we read that He was sent on a mission for a distinct purpose. Even as a boy of twelve He knew that He must be about His Father's business. Later, Jesus said, "I have finished the work which thou gavest me to do" (John 17:4). When the mission was accomplished, He cried out, "It is finished!" (John 19:30).

His mission was to take men who were dead in trespasses and sins and to transform them so that "we might live through him" (I John 4:9). And by the way, the life which God gives through Him is *everlasting life.* The moment a child is born into the world, he is under the sentence of death. We were all born with the seed of death in us. Jesus came into the world that men might live forever, that we might live through *HIM.* This is the great theme of the Gospel through John.

"In Him was life" (John 1:4).

". . . should not perish, but have everlasting life" (John 3:16).

"The water that I shall give him shall be in him a well of water springing up into everlasting life" (John 4:14).

"He that heareth my word, and believeth on him that sent me, hath everlasting life, and shall not come into condemnation; but is passed from death unto life" (John 5:24).

"If any man eat of this bread, he shall live forever" (John 6:51).

"If a man keep my saying, he shall never see death" (John 8:51).

"I am come that they might have life, and that they might have it more abundantly" (John 10:10).

"I am the resurrection, and the life" (John 11:25).

"I am the way, the truth, and the life" (John 14:6).

"These are written, that ye might believe that Jesus is the Christ, the Son of God; and that believing ye might have life through his name" (John 20:31).

This is the glorious answer to a human race that was under the sentence of eternal death. This is the answer to the question of the ages. Job, centuries ago, said there is hope for the tree, for if it is cut down, it will sprout again. But he wondered about man. "If a man die, shall he live again?" (Job 14:14). The answer is that we have life through union with Jesus Christ. Christ means eternal life, abundant life, satisfying life, resurrection life, indwelling life. Not to have Christ means not to have life. *In Him is life.*

How can we live forever when we were born in sin? Not only do we need life but we also need to be rid of our sins. A man cannot stand in the presence of God when he is sinful. John gives us the answer.

He loved us, and sent his Son to be the propitiation for our sins (I John 4:10).

He sent His Son as a sacrifice to put away sin at the cross. He is the propitiation, the satisfaction, for our sins. *God is satisfied.*

"Behold the Lamb of God, which taketh away the sin of the world" (John 1:29).

" . . . When he had by himself purged our sins, sat down on the right hand of the Majesty on high" (Heb. 1:3).

"Without shedding of blood is no remission" (Heb. 9:22).

"But this man, after he had offered one sacrifice for sins for ever, sat down on the right hand of God" (Heb. 10:12).

"For by one offering he hath perfected for ever them that are sanctified" (Heb. 10:14).

"All we like sheep have gone astray; we have turned every one to his own way; and the Lord hath laid on him the iniquity of us all" (Isa. 53:6).

"Who his own self bare our sins in his own body on the tree, that we, being dead to sins, should live unto righteousness: by whose stripes ye were healed" (I Pet. 2:24).

"And ye know that he was manifested to take away our sins; and in him is no sin" (I John 3:5).

"Now once in the end of the world hath he appeared to put away sin by the sacrifice of himself" (Heb. 9:26). "World" should be translated "age."

How could I possibly have eternal life when I am dead in sins? Something must happen to those sins. Either I must die for them or someone else must die in my place. Isn't it wonderful that He came not only to give us life but also to put away sin by the sacrifice of Himself? No one can ever produce any evidence in the presence of God to show that a believer has ever sinned. You see, our Saviour didn't just cover our sins. He put them away, once, for all, forever.

"By his own blood he entered in once into the holy place, having obtained eternal redemption for us" (Heb. 9:12).

"One sacrifice for sins for ever" (Heb. 10:12).

"So Christ was once offered to bear the sins of many; and unto them that look for him shall he appear the second time without sin unto salvation" (Heb. 9:28).

He came the first time to put away sin. He came the first time to make provision whereby we might be fitted for the presence of God. He came the first time as the Lamb of God who takes away the sin of the world.

He is coming again, and then it will be to judge sinners. In flaming fire He is going to take vengeance on them that know not God (II Thess. 1:8). When He comes the second time, the Lamb of God will be the Judge.

Have you accepted Him? He became an accursed thing so that you might be saved. My yearning is that you might have a tremendous love for the Saviour. May your love be so great and so wonderful that people will be attracted to the One who put away sin, so that they may receive the Saviour and pass from death to life.

ASSURANCE OF OUR UNION WITH HIM

How can we know that we are in union with the Saviour? How can we know that we are in fellowship with God who is love? The apostle gives to us four definite assurances.

1. We know because of our love for His people.

> **Beloved, if God so loved us, we ought also to love one another.**
>
> **No man hath seen God at any time. If we love one another, God dwelleth in us, and his love is perfected in us (I John 4:11,12).**

Our relationship with God makes us right in our relationship with men. I can know that I am in right relationship with God when I am in right relationship with my brethren. One is the outflow of the other. Our love for God is displayed by our love for the brethren. If this is not true, then love is just an empty word.

God did not start to love us when we accepted Jesus Christ as Saviour. He loved us when we were sinners. He loved us when we hated Him, when we were afar from Him, when we were dead in trespasses and sins, without Christ, without hope, without God. He demonstrated His love by sacrifice, and He gave His Son to die for us. When we accept the Saviour, that same love which gave His Son to die for us is manifested through us to others. *Our love for God is displayed by obedience to His Word. Our love for each other is displayed by sacrifice.* This is the recurring theme through the Epistle of John.

2. *We know because He has given to us His Spirit.*

> **Hereby know we that we dwell in him, and he in us, because he hath given us of his Spirit (I John 4:13).**

There are other Scriptures which state that the Spirit of God dwells in the believer in Jesus Christ, the Incarnate Word of God. "And I will pray the Father, and he shall give you another Comforter, that he may abide with you for ever; Even the Spirit of truth; whom the world cannot receive, because it seeth him not, neither knoweth him: but ye know him: for he dwelleth with you, and shall be in you" (John 14:16,17).

"Know ye not that ye are the temple of God, and that the Spirit of God dwelleth in you?" (I Cor. 3:16).

"What? know ye not that your body is the temple of the Holy Ghost which is in you, which ye have of God, and ye are not your own?" (I Cor. 6:19).

"And hereby we know that he abideth in us, by the Spirit which he hath given us" (I John 3:24).

By our love for others we know that "the love of God is shed abroad in our hearts by the Holy Ghost which is given unto us" (Rom 5:5). Remember, *God sees my faith, but men experience my love.* As we walk with God, His love is perfected in us so that the character of God is revealed through us in our actions toward others. The very fact that we love the people of God evidences that we are walking in fellowship with God. The ability to love must come from God Himself and is one of the fruits of the Spirit of God in His people. "The fruit of the Spirit is love, joy, peace, longsuffering, gentleness, goodness, faith, meekness, temperance: against such there is no law" (Gal. 5:22,23).

Someone has stated it this way: the fruit of the Spirit is love manifested by joy, peace, longsuffering, etc. This is divine love. If we truly love God, then we will have divine love in our hearts and lives, and there will be a display of that love by obedience to His Word and by sacrifice for others.

When our Lord was living among men, He said, "He that hath seen me hath seen the Father" (John 14:9). John said, "No man hath seen God at any time; the only begotten Son; which is in the bosom of the Father, he hath declared him" (John 1:18). How are men going to see God today? How are men going to know that God is love today? It must be through His people! This is not just theory, this is real life. When we come into the experience of life in Christ, His life is demonstrated through us by the Spirit of God who indwells us. This produces our obedience to His Word and our love for the brethren, a love which is willing to sacrifice one for the other. This is our assurance. This is how we know that we are in fellowship with God who is love.

3. We know because of our confession of His Person.

> And we have seen and do testify that the Father sent the Son to be the Saviour of the world.
>
> Whosoever shall confess that Jesus is the Son of God, God dwelleth in Him, and he in God (I John 4:14,15).

The value of the cross of Christ is dependent upon *who* died on that cross. It was not just a man who died for us, but it was the Son of God. The very fact that we testify that it was God's Son whom God sent into the world to be the Saviour of sinners is evidence of our union with God, evidence of our life in Him. The Spirit of God in us is displayed through our love of God and our love of the brethren and our confession that Jesus is the Son of God. This gives us our assurance.

4. We know because we are dwelling in His love.

> **And we have known and believed the love that God hath to us. God is love; and he that dwelleth in love dwelleth in God, and God in him.**
>
> **Herein is our love made perfect, that we may have boldness in the day of judgment: because as he is, so are we in this world.**
>
> **There is no fear in love; but perfect love casteth out fear: because fear hath torment. He that feareth is not made perfect in love.**
>
> **We love him, because he first loved us (I John 4:16-19).**

What a wonderful, wonderful truth this is! When we accepted Jesus Christ as our Saviour, we were joined to Him in an intimate union. We have been made partakers of life, His divine life. We are joined to the Son of God. God never for one moment sees us without His Son. When we stand in the presence of God, we stand in all the beauty and righteousness and glory of Christ. What an assurance this union gives for the life of the believer!

One of the great purposes of redemption was that God might have a people with whom He could have fellowship. Did you ever think of the anticipation of God when His children are ready for glory? "Precious in the sight of the LORD is the death of his saints" (Psa. 116:15). God is anxious for them, waiting for them to come home. God has forgiven them, saved them, given them eternal life, made them His children. They have been tested and tried and refined while upon earth. God has used them in one way or another for the glorifying of His person and for the manifestation of His grace and His love and His compassion. And then He brings them home. Isn't this cause for assurance?

Think on these things. Lay hold of the assurance God gives to us. We know we have His life abiding in us, not only an imparted life but also an imparted love. We know we have His Spirit dwelling in us. We know we love Him and love His people. We know we belong to Him by our confession of Christ as our own Saviour. We know we have union with God. We dwell in love because God is love. We dwell in God and God in us and so we dwell in love.

The *result* of this should be a boldness before God. Perfect love has made provision for the believer to have confidence and boldness in the presence of God.

> **Herein is our love made perfect, that we may have boldness in the day of judgment: because as he is, so are we in this world (I John 4:17).**

We find this same thought in the book of Hebrews. "Let us therefore come boldly unto the throne of grace, that we may obtain mercy, and find grace to help in time of need" (Heb. 4:16). We who are creatures of the dust can have real, intimate fellowship with God.

Divine love, imparted to us, guarantees the perfection of His purpose in His people. We have three glorious proofs of love making perfect. Let us look at them.

In chapter two, we found that because we love Him and belong to Him we live in obedience to His Word. "But whoso keepeth his word, in Him verily is the love of God perfected: hereby know we that we are in him" (I John 2:5). *This is in our relationship to God.*

In chapter four, we found that His love is perfected in us in our manifestation of love for the people of God. "If we love one another, God dwelleth in us, and his love is perfected in us" (I John 4:12). *This is in our relationship to others.*

Here, in I John 4:17, we find that our love is made perfect that we may have boldness in the day of judgment. We have peace of heart and all fear is gone. *This is in our relationship to self.*

Notice, it does not say as He is, so will we be when we get to heaven. We all would believe that. The Bible clearly states that when we see Him, we shall be like Him (I John 3:2). God has determined that we are going to be conformed to the image of His Son (Rom. 8:29). Oh yes, when we get to heaven, we will never fail Him. But this verse 17 is saying that just as He is, so are we now. In this world! This is our *position in Christ.* This is our relationship. Death, sin, judgment are all behind us. No one can produce any evidence in the presence of God that we were sinners. His perfect love has made a perfect provision for us to come into His presence. Hence, we have boldness.

Death, sin, judgment are all in the past. When we stand before God, we stand before Him without sin. We stand in the righteousness of Christ. This gives us peace of heart, boldness, confidence. God has made a marvelous provision for us in His Son, and it is beyond the comprehension of men. If we wait until we can analyze and understand all the program and purpose of God in man's redemption, we will wait until it is too late. In fact, one cannot know until one first accepts the Saviour. When we accept Jesus Christ, the door is flung open by the Spirit of God, and He keeps and guides us into all truth. He makes the things of Christ very real to us.

I love this 17th verse. It was one of the first verses I learned when I became a Christian. It was so beyond me I could hardly believe that it was in the Bible. Yet, here it stands in the Word of God. "As He is, so are we in this world."

Someone may ask why I don't talk about Christian service. Doesn't that come in here somewhere? Service is the outflow of our fellowship with the Saviour, our relationship to Him. The more we walk with Him, the more gladly we serve Him. Otherwise we get occupied with self, become indifferent to Him, and service becomes a burden. It is so easy for all of us to allow things to interfere with our own intimate fellowship with God and our walk with Him. Yet this should always be our first concern.

The perfect provision that God has made for us, whereby we can fully enjoy that fellowship with Him, is that "perfect love casteth out fear." Christianity is not a religion of fear. I recognize there are those who try to scare people into obedience to God by calling the judgment and wrath of God upon them. I find so many Christians who are fearful about coming into the presence of God, not sure about their eternal destiny. The reason they are not sure is that they look at themselves, their works, their service, their failures. They become so occupied with their weaknesses that they are miserable. There is a terrible fruitage from self-occupation and introspection. Not only does it produce selfishness and egotism but also discouragement. By the way, Satan doesn't mind a bit if we get occupied with ourselves and our accomplishments. Our accomplishments may make us proud and our failures may make us discouraged. Satan doesn't care which it is, so long as we are not occupied with the Saviour. When we get our eyes on Christ, we find the One whom God accepts, and we are accepted in the Beloved.

God never sees us apart from His Son. In Christ we can have perfect peace. "Peace I leave with you, my peace I give unto you: not as the world giveth, give I unto you. Let not your heart be troubled, neither let it be afraid" (John 14:27).

"These things I have spoken unto you, that in me ye might have peace. In the world ye shall have tribulation: but be of good cheer; I have overcome the world" (John 16:33).

"He is our peace" (Eph. 2:14).

"And the very God of peace sanctify you wholly; and I pray God your whole spirit and soul and body be preserved blameless unto the coming of our Lord Jesus Christ. Faithful is he that calleth you, who also will do it" (I Thess. 5:23,24).

Fear and love do not go together. The more we look at ourselves and at each other, the more we find fault and become fearful. The more we love the Saviour and are occupied with Him, the more we will experience perfect peace. Let us read the Word of God to see the Saviour, to understand what kind of Father we have, and to know His provision for all our needs. Then love will replace our fears. Perfect peace and full joy is found in Jesus Christ, our wonderful Saviour.

LOVE MANIFESTED IN HIS CHILDREN

We love Him because He first loved us. Love responds to love. We love the brethren because He commanded us to do so and we manifest our love to God by our obedience to His command.

> If a man say, I love God, and hateth his brother, he is a liar: for he that loveth not his brother whom he hath seen, how can he love God whom he hath not seen?
>
> And this commandment have we from him, That he who loveth God love his brother also (I John 4:20,21).

Let us note this very carefully. In John 15:15-17 Jesus *calls* us to be friends. He has *chosen* us, and ordained us, that we should go and bring forth fruit. He *commands* us to love one another as He has loved us. Don't twist these around. We must love the people of God because He commands it. If we love Him, we will love His children.

Satan takes great delight in breaking up the assemblies of God's people by destroying their love the one for the other. I'm sorry to say that we see bitterness, envy, jealousy even among God's wonderful people. Churches have been broken, not because of their love for the truth, but because of personalities. Yet, we know that the Lord always loves us. Even though we are in frailty, weakness, and failure, His love for us is not affected. Now Jesus commands us to love the brethren just as He loves us.

Our reaction is to say that such love is impossible for us. It is a supernatural love. That is correct. But Romans 5:5 tells us that divine love has been shed abroad in our hearts by the Holy Spirit. It was noted that in the early church they loved one another. Cannot we demonstrate this same love? If we do not love the brother whom we have seen, how can we love God whom we have not seen?

Our next reaction may be to say we just don't feel like it. That also may be true. Then we should go look in the mirror and marvel at the grace of God that He could love even us. Love covers a multitude of sins (I Pet. 4:8). Instead of criticizing and judging people, we are to love them. God has given us that divine love by His Spirit so that we can manifest supernatural love. We manifest our love for the Saviour by loving the people of God—the "ornery" as well as the lovely ones, regardless of age or circumstance or experience. If we have trouble doing that, then let us get on our knees and pray for them.

Another way in which we may try to excuse ourselves is that we may be inclined to rationalize by asking who is our brother. John immediately goes on to define this for us.

> **Whosoever believeth that Jesus is the Christ is born of God: and every one that loveth him that begat loveth him also that is begotten of him (I John 5:1).**

The basis of our brotherhood, of our fellowship, is *divine life*. Ecclesiastical distinctions are not the basis. Anyone who loves the Lord Jesus Christ is a brother. Notice it states that a brother is whosoever believes that Jesus is the Christ, the Anointed of God. It is the Christ who died, who was sent to be the propitiation for our sins. May I say again, the importance of the cross is *who* died on the cross. The brethren are those who are trusting the work of the Christ who died on the cross. Everyone who believes that Jesus is the Christ and accepts Him as his own personal Saviour is born of God. That is divine life. Being born of God, he will love God; and, loving God, he will love the *people* of God. The reality of divine life is seen in obedience to His commandment.

All who have put their trust in the Saviour have the same life, the same salvation, the same faith, the same love, the same standing, the same relationship. Now it is true that one may have a weak faith and another a strong faith, but whoever confesses Christ as Saviour belongs to His family. We may have different shades of doctrine, but that does not mean that we should not love one another, nor does it mean that we cannot have fellowship together. According to Ephesians 4:1-6 there is a unity of the Spirit based on the foundation of one body, one Lord, one faith, one baptism, one God and Father of all. If we believe that Jesus Christ is the Son of God, that He is God manifest in the flesh, that He died to put away our sins by the sacrifice of Himself, that He was buried, that He was raised from the dead with the body that was nailed to the cross, that He has gone back to heaven to be a Prince and a Saviour, that He will return to the earth and will reign in power and great glory, then we are brothers!

"Every one that loveth him that begat loveth him also that is begotten of him." If we love God, we will love the children of God, all those who are born of God. This is what Jesus said, "By this shall all men know that ye are my disciples, if ye have love one to another" (John 13:35). The outflow of our love for the Saviour is our love for the brethren. Remember, God sees our faith but men experience our love. Our love for God is manifested by obedience, but our love for other Christians is manifested by sacrifice.

God has given us the responsibility of loving the people of God and of obeying the Word of God, but we *experience* divine life and fellowship with God when we love the people of God and when we obey His Word. So John uses that word "know" again.

> By this we know that we love the children of God, when we love God, and keep his commandments (I John 5:2).

Now John goes on to explain about the commandments of God.

> For this is the love of God, that we keep his commandments: and his commandments are not grievous (I John 5:3).

The man out of Christ has his tests, his sorrows, his trials, his sufferings, his disappointments, his afflictions. On whom can he lean? Where can he turn? What hope does he have when he faces death, the last enemy of man?

Many people are afraid to become a Christian because they fear they might have to give up certain things. They are afraid they cannot do certain things or go certain places. Our verse tells us, however, that this is the love of God that we keep His Word, and His Word is not grievous. It never becomes a burden. Christians also go through their tests and trials and sorrows, but there is a difference. Christians have an imparted divine life and an imparted divine love. The one who has accepted the Saviour faces his tests in union with the living God.

The possibility is that the more closely one walks with God in this world, the more tests and trials that person will have. It is through the tests and trials that the believer experiences the power of God and learns to know His ways, His tenderness, His compassion. Those tests, trials, and afflictions become open doors for God to demonstrate His love, His power, His grace, His concern for us.

We have a Saviour who understands every test of life. "For in that he himself hath suffered being tempted, he is able to succour them that are tempted" (Heb. 2:18).

"Let us therefore come boldly unto the throne of grace, that we may obtain mercy, and find grace to help in time of need" (Heb. 4:16). Remember that it was in the storm that the disciples learned about the Christ whom they were following. "What manner of man is this, that even the winds and the sea obey him!" (Matt. 8:27).

When people object to Christianity by saying it demands that we give up too many pleasant things, I ask them, "Where do you find that in the Bible?" I am afraid people think that the commandments which the Lord Jesus mentions and that John speaks of here are the Law of Moses. Please, let *us* not put people under the bondage of a Mosaic economy. This is not what John has in mind here. Peter is speaking of the Law of Moses when he says, "Now therefore why tempt ye God, to put a yoke upon the neck of the disciples, which neither our fathers nor we were able to bear?" (Acts 15:10). The commandments of our Saviour are not grievous. "Come unto me, all ye that labour and are heavy laden, and I will give you rest. Take my yoke upon you, and learn of me; for I am meek and lowly in heart: and ye shall find rest unto your souls. For my yoke is easy, and my burden is light" (Matt. 11:28-30).

Faith not only appropriates Christ for salvation but it appropriates Christ for victory.

> **For whatsoever is born of God overcometh the world: and this is the victory that overcometh the world, even our faith.**
>
> **Who is he that overcometh the world, but he that believeth that Jesus is the Son of God? (I John 5:4,5).**

This reminds us of the words of our Lord: "These things I have spoken unto you, that in me ye might have peace.

In the world ye shall have tribulation: but be of good cheer; I have overcome the world" (John 16:33). It also reminds us of a little song.

> **Cheer up, ye saints of God, there's nothing to worry about,**
>> **Nothing to make you feel afraid, nothing to make you doubt.**
>
> **Remember, Jesus never fails, so why not trust Him and shout?**
>> **You'll be sorry you worried at all tomorrow morning!**

We have already learned about the world in I John 2:15-17 where we read, "Love not the world, neither the things that are in the world . . . " The world is a system that is diametrically opposed to God. It is a religious, economic, social, political system, and God is not the center of it at all. In the realm of religion, Satan is its god (II Cor. 4:4). In the realm of government, Satan is its prince (John 12:31, John 14:30, John 16:11). We are living in an enemy world.

Then how can we overcome the world? We will find that the harder we struggle, the firmer we set our will, the more we try to do in the energy of the flesh, the more failure we experience. We are given the answer here, and it is a simple answer. "Whosoever is born of God overcometh the world." Our Saviour is none other than the Lord from heaven. Victory over the world is guaranteed to us through Jesus Christ our Saviour.

Allow me to take the time here to make a comparison between verses one and five. When John is defining who the brethren are, he says, "Whosoever believeth that Jesus is the Christ" (I John 5:1). This has reference to the work on the cross. Remember, the important issue is: Who died on the cross? When the Spirit of God speaks about the work of our Saviour on the cross, He makes it clear it is the Christ who died, The Anointed One of God. This refers to *His work.*

When John is stating who it is that has the victory and overcomes the world, he says, "He that believeth that Jesus is the Son of God" (I John 5:5). This refers to *His Person.* Notice that when the Spirit of God is talking about the Lordship of our Saviour, it is Jesus, the Son of God. God the Father raised up this Jesus, who had been crucified, and exalted Him to be a Prince and a Saviour (Acts 5:30,31). He is the resurrected One, the glorified One. Our faith is in a Saviour who is the Lord over all, and victory is guaranteed to us because He is victorious over death, the grave, and Satan.

Who is the one who overcomes? He is the one who is willing to confess that Jesus is risen and exalted on the throne, that He is none other than the Son of God. "Nay, in all these things we are more than conquerors through him that loved us" (Rom. 8:37). The overcomer is in relationship and union with the Son of God and realizes that He has already obtained the victory for us. The overcomer knows that the Son of God defeated Satan at the cross and robbed death of its fear and has become the life of His people.

John is the only one who talks about being an overcomer. He talks about this in his letters to the seven churches in Revelation 1—3, and he mentions it here in his Epistle. There are those who say that the overcomer is the believer overcoming sin and Satan and the world. They talk about living a victorious life. However, John is careful to explain the words he uses and to tell us what they mean.

An example of John explaining his use of a word is in the word "abide." "And he that keepeth his commandments dwelleth in him, and he in him. And hereby we know that he abideth in us, by the Spirit which he hath given us" (I John 3:24). In the Gospel of John we are told what it means to "abide." "If ye keep my commandments, ye shall abide in my love; even as I have kept my Father's commandments, and abide in his love" (John 15:10). It is true that to abide means to be in fellowship with God. But who is the one who is in fellowship? It is the one who is obedient!

So here John is careful to explain who is an overcomer. "Who is he that overcometh the world, but he that believeth that Jesus is the Son of God?" (I John 5:5). We overcome all obstacles through Him that loved us (Rom. 8:37-39). We overcome the enemy of our souls through the Spirit of God who indwells us, and He is greater than he who is in the world. It is the indwelling Spirit of God who guarantees victory over the enemy (I John 4:1-6). We overcome all obstacles because of relationship with the Son of God. It is faith in His Person, believing and confessing that Jesus is the Son of God, that is the mark of an overcomer (I John 5:4,5).

Peter and James do not use the word "overcomer." They both do speak of the fact that in faith we are to resist the devil. Resist the devil and *he* will do the fleeing, not you. "Be sober, be vigilant; because your adversary the devil, as a roaring lion, walketh about, seeking whom he may devour: Whom resist stedfast in the faith, knowing that the same afflictions are accomplished in your brethren that are in the world" (I Pet. 5:8,9). "Submit yourselves therefore to God. Resist the devil, and he will flee from you" (James 4:7). Faith makes victory possible. Love makes it easy. It delights the heart of God.

This is really the end of the discussion, or we may call it the argument, of the Epistle. We have learned that we have fellowship with God who is light. This is the description of His character. We have fellowship with God who is righteous, righteous not only in His character but also in His works. We have fellowship with God who is love. How can we *know* that we belong to God who is love? We know that we are in fellowship with Him because of our union with Him, because of our love for the brethren, because of our obedience to His Word, because we have victory over the world. Our attitude to the brethren is to be one of love; our attitude to the Word of God is to be obedience;

our attitude to the world is to be one of victory. This gives us the assurance of our fellowship with the eternal God. What more do we need?

Throughout the entire Epistle the great yearning of the Spirit of God and the theme of the whole book is that we might have intimate, personal daily fellowship with God. God wants us to really believe what He says, wants us to trust Him, and wants us to be obedient to His Word. He wants each of us to say, "I know whom I have believed, and am persuaded that he is able to keep that which I have committed unto him against that day" (II Tim. 1:12). Permit me to give a paraphrase of this: "I know whom I have believed and am persuaded that He is able to guard the deposit which I have made with Him against that day."

The close of the Epistle gives us the results of fellowship with such a God. There are divine assurances which God Himself gives to us. There are certain truths which are absolutely immoveable and unchangeable because these assurances come from God, and He is the One who stands behind them. We overcome the world through the Saviour. *Jesus Christ gets the victory and we enjoy the deliverance.*

The truth stands that if you have accepted Jesus Christ as your Saviour, then this wonderful God, who is light and love and righteousness, makes Himself responsible for you. He is responsible that your faith will continue; He makes Himself responsible that your love will be enlarged; He makes it His responsibility that you will stand before Him in all the beauty of Christ. He simply asks you to believe, to put your trust, in this wonderful Saviour.

DIVINE
CERTAINTIES
AND
ASSURANCES

This is he that came by water and blood, even Jesus Christ; not by water only, but by water and blood. And it is the Spirit that beareth witness, because the Spirit is truth.

For there are three that bear record in heaven, the Father, the Word, and the Holy Ghost: and these three are one.

And there are three that bear witness in earth, the Spirit, and the water, and the blood: and these three agree in one (I John 5:6-8).

CERTAINTY OF GOD'S TESTIMONY

We have come now to a difficult portion of Scripture. There are varying interpretations of these verses and so one cannot be dogmatic about them. However, I would say that the key word in the passage is "witness." In verse six it is "the Spirit that beareth witness." In verse seven "there are three that bear record (or witness) in heaven." In verse eight "there are three that bear witness in earth." In other words, we are dealing here with the question of God's testimony, God's witness. This witness is certain. God is the witness to the person and work of His Son.

It is remarkable to note that our Saviour's ministry started at the River Jordan when He was baptized in water and ended at the cross where He shed His blood. I do not know exactly what is the mind of the Spirit concerning these two but I can make suggestions for you to follow through.

"This is He that came by water and blood, even Jesus Christ; not by water only, but by water and blood." John 19:34,35 tells us that when our Lord was crucified, the Roman soldier took his spear and pierced His side and forthwith there came out water and blood. The Spirit of God bears witness to this fact.

However, in these verses I would like to suggest that the *water* has to do with *moral* cleansing for power, for the Christian walk, for witness. This is the *manward* side of the Christian life. The *blood* speaks of *judicial* cleansing. This is the cleansing of our sins *before God.* We need always to remember that it is not our value of the blood of Christ that saves us, but it is that great value that God has placed on the blood of His Son that saves us. "Without the shedding of blood is no remission" (Heb. 9:22).

In the New Testament quite often the water is spoken of as a term referring to the Word of God and is used for moral cleansing. "Now ye are clean through the word which I have spoken unto you" (John 15:3). In Ephesians 5:26 it states that Christ sanctifies and cleanses the church "with the washing of water by the word." The words "water" and "word" are also used for life in Christ, for relationship to the Son of God. In John 4 there can be no life apart from the Water of Life. "The water that I shall give him shall be in him a well of water springing up into everlasting life" (John 4:14). Peter says that we are born again "not of corruptible seed, but of incorruptible, by the word of God, which liveth and abideth for ever" (I Peter

1:23). James tells us the same thing: "Of his own will begat he us with the word of truth" (James 1:18).

The Spirit of God is bearing testimony to the fact that this Jesus is the One who came by water and came by blood. The water speaks of the reception of life and of the moral cleansing through the Word. The blood speaks of the judicial cleansing which gives us our standing before God on the ground of the shed blood of Christ.

Then notice that there are three who bear record in heaven: the Father, the Word, and the Holy Ghost. These three are one. This verse is not included in some translations of the Bible because according to some of the Greek scholars this verse was not in the original manuscripts. Be that as it may, there is here the unity of witness in the Godhead. The Father, the Son, and the Holy Ghost are one.

In verse eight the witness here on earth is stated. The Spirit of God, the water (Word of God), and the blood (the sacrifice of Christ) agree in one. One cannot read the Bible without recognizing that the Spirit of God uses the Word of God in an open heart and thus brings the water of life freely to those who will receive it. "For our gospel came not unto you in word only, but also in power, and in the Holy Ghost, and in much assurance" (I Thess. 1:5). We have received for ourselves and we preach the gospel of the redemption which is in Christ Jesus, that is, the blood of Christ shed for us. We use the Word of God to receive the testimony of the Saviour for ourselves and we use it to bring men to Christ. The Spirit of God takes that Word and makes it to be a living reality in any open heart.

Don't try to be mystical about the divine testimony in verses six to eight. Simply take the facts. Christ came. He poured out His life for us and His precious blood was shed. The Spirit of God, in fact, the living God Himself, Father, Son, and Spirit, bear testimony to the fact that there is no other way of salvation but in Christ Jesus.

CERTAINTY OF ETERNAL LIFE

If we receive the witness of men, the witness of God is greater: for this is the witness of God which he hath testified of his Son (I John 5:9).

This verse forms a transition between the certainty of God's witness and the certainty of eternal life. The Word of God is greater than the word of men. How easy it is for us to accept the word of men. We go to school and read textbooks written by men and if the scholars agree on some point, we accept their witness. Then why do we approach the Word of God with such a big question mark? Why is it so much easier for people to accept the witness of men than to accept the witness of God?

One of the tragedies of our country and of so-called churches of Jesus Christ is the fact that the Word of God is questioned. Mark this! If the Bible is not the Word of God, then we have absolutely no revelation of the heart and character of God. We cannot know what He is, or who He is, or any of His purpose. Let us be very realistic about this. We can turn to creation and say that there must be a God because of the argument of design. But to know God we must have the revelation of Scriptures.

John is saying in this verse that God is giving a witness concerning His Son. Are we going to believe what He says or are we going to question it? Some folk will say that to believe it is just blind faith. No, my friend, there is no such thing as blind faith. *Faith must have an object, otherwise it isn't faith.* The important thing is not faith but the object of faith. Are we going to believe God's Word or not? "This is the witness of God."

Do not say, "I am going to try to believe it." That is an insult! Not believe God? How could one dare question His character and His veracity? There is no middle ground; one either believes Him or one does not. God has spoken in no uncertain way concerning His Son and concerning the salvation He has provided for men and women. He has spoken concerning the eternal future, concerning His dealing with the nations of the earth, concerning His plan for Israel, concerning His work for the church. He has spoken concerning you and me. And now here is His testimony:

> He that believeth on the Son of God hath the witness in himself: he that believeth not God hath made him a liar; because he believeth not the record that God gave of his Son.
>
> And this is the record, that God hath given to us eternal life, and this life is in his Son.
>
> He that hath the Son hath life; and he that hath not the Son of God hath not life (I John 5:10-12).

When God speaks, He speaks concerning His Son. God's great theme and the delight of His heart are concerning His Son. At the baptism of Jesus, God said, "This is my beloved Son, in whom I am well pleased" (Matt. 3:17). In Matthew 17 at the transfiguration, God said, "This is my beloved Son, in whom I am well pleased; hear ye him." He is saying in effect, "Never mind Moses and never mind Elijah. My Son has come. Hear Him!" Hebrews 1:2 tells us that He "hath in these last days spoken unto us by His Son." We must listen to what the Son has to say because God is speaking to us through Jesus Christ, His Son. If we spurn what the Son of God has said, then we are spurning the Word of God.

God holds us responsible to believe what He has said. He does not ask us to *understand* everything that He has said, but He does want us to *believe* everything that He has said. We should never doubt that God has spoken to us through His Son. Christ's words, His life, His actions and attitudes, the very purpose for which He came, all substantiate this. As a young boy He said, "Wist ye not that I must be about my Father's business?" (Luke 2:49). At the end of His life He could say, "I have finished the *WORK* that You gave

Me to do . . . I have given to them the *WORDS* which You gave Me" (John 17:4,8).

We are responsible to hear what His Son has to say. God is not speaking by means of angels or dreams. He has given to us a Bible to read, and in that Word by the Spirit of God there is revealed the character, the work, and the person of His Son. The Father is witnessing to us through the Son. If we want to know God, we must know Him through the Son. If we want to come to God, we must come to Him through the Son. Jesus Christ, the Incarnate Word of God, is the one Mediator between God and men (I Tim. 2:5).

If you accept God's blessed Son as your own personal Saviour, if you believe the record that God has given concerning His Son, then you are brought into relationship with Him. You have become the child of One who is God. To be an obedient child of God, we must know what He says. Not to believe what God has said about His Son is to make God a liar. Remember that Romans 3:4 tells us, "Let God be true, but every man a liar."

"He that believeth on the Son of God hath the witness in himself." The Spirit of God comes to indwell that person and reveals to that person the wonderful glories of our Saviour. God sent His Son to redeem them that were under the law, so we might receive the adoption of sons, and, because we are sons, God has sent forth the Spirit of His Son into our hearts (Gal. 4:4-7). As many as are led by the Spirit of God, they are the sons of God . . . The Spirit bears witness with our spirit, that we are the children of God (Rom. 8:14-16). When we accept the Saviour, our bodies become the sanctuary of the Holy Spirit. A new thing happens in our lives, and our desires are changed. This is one of the confirmations by God to the believer, through the Spirit, that he has become the child of One who is God.

Let us note in review that according to I John 2 we know we have life because we keep His Word. In chapter 3, we know we have life because we love the brethren. In chapter 5 we know we have eternal life because we believe His Word.

"And this is the record, that God hath given to us eternal life, and this life is in his Son." This is *eternal life,* not life for five or 10 or even 60 years. If you have put your trust in the Saviour but you do not believe that you have eternal life, you are making God a liar.

This eternal life, is an imparted life, a communicated life. This life is in His Son. "He that hath the Son hath life." "The wages of sin is death; but the gift of God is eternal life through Jesus Christ our Lord" (Romans 6:23).

"In Him was life" (John 1:4).

"He that believeth on the Son hath everlasting life" (John 3:36).

In studying the Gospel of John we find that this imparted, communicated life which He gives to us is not only eternal life, but it is satisfying life according to John 6:35 and 4:14. It is a life over which death has no power because it is a resurrected life (John 6:39-44). It is an indwelling life (John 6:53-58). It is an abundant life (John 10:10). This life is in Christ Jesus because He is the Life (John 14:6). This is the record that God has given. Eternal life is in His Son.

Let us say very frankly that there are a great, great many Christians who are not *enjoying* their salvation but are *enduring* it. They are full of fear that they might lose their salvation and lose their life in Christ. In other words, they do not believe that they have *eternal* life. They have accepted the Saviour and they are saved, but they are uninstructed. They do not understand the completeness of the work of Christ at the cross. When a Christian does not believe with certainty that he has eternal life, he is casting a shadow on the work of Christ at the cross. "By his own blood he entered in ONCE into the holy place, having obtained an ETERNAL redemption for us" (Heb. 9:12).

When you were redeemed by the precious blood of

Christ, it was an eternal work which God performed. You may not now *experience* all that salvation means, but the life you possess is an eternal life, and the salvation you possess is a complete salvation. "Being confident of this very thing, that He which hath begun a good work in you will perform it until the day of Jesus Christ" (Phil. 1:6). "To perform in this verse means "to perfect it." "I know that, whatsoever God doeth, it shall be forever" (Eccl. 3:14).

Please do not dishonor the Son of God and the work He did for you. Do not make God to be a liar by accepting the Saviour and then doubting that you have eternal life. Do not deny the completeness of the work of Christ at the cross. Remember it is not your value of the work of Christ at the cross but it is the great value which God has placed on the work of His Son which gives it efficacy. When Christ died on the cross, He did a complete job. He put away our sins and forgave every one of our sins. He defeated the powers of hell and the dominion of death and the grave. *We enjoy a complete salvation because we have a complete Saviour.*

"He that hath the Son hath life." The difference between life and death is Jesus Christ, the Son of God. If you have accepted Jesus Christ as your own personal Saviour, you have eternal life and eternal glory and will spend all eternity in the presence of God.

The Son of God is mentioned eight times in verses one to thirteen. God is well pleased in His Son. He has made provision for our salvation in His Son and He has also made provision for us to be kept in that salvation. Romans 5:1-11 teaches that the tests and trials of life do not destroy faith but purify and strengthen faith. The very love of God is the guarantee that the faith which He has given to us will never fail. I may fail and you may fail just as Peter failed, but faith does not fail. The Lord expressly prayed for Peter so that his *faith* would not fail (Luke 22:32).

"Wherefore He is able also to save them to the uttermost that come unto God by Him" (Heb. 7:25). He is able to save perfectly everyone who comes to God through Jesus Christ.

"He that hath the Son hath life; and he that hath not the Son of God hath not life."

Unbelief in the Son of God and rejection of His Person and of His work leave nothing but outer darkness. "He that believeth not the Son shall not see life; but the wrath of God abideth on him" (John 3:36). Jesus said that whoever does not believe that He is the "I AM" shall die in his sins (John 8:24). "It is appointed unto men once to die, but after this the judgment" (Heb. 9:27). Those who deny the living God shall never see light (Psa. 49:16-20). How terrible! Such a man will live eternally in darkness.

God is light (I John 1:5). If a man spurn the God who is light, then there can be nothing left but darkness. The difference between light and darkness has nothing to do with being good or bad, being religious or irreligious. The difference lies in personal relationship with Christ Jesus, the Son of God.

God has borne testimony to His Son by raising Him from the dead. God has appointed a day in which He will judge the world in righteousness by that Man whom He has ordained; whereof He has given assurance unto all men, in that He has raised Him from the dead (Acts 17:31). God has marked Jesus Christ, the Son of God, out from everybody else by the resurrection from the dead (Rom. 1:3,4). The resurrection of Jesus Christ is God's personal testimony that this One who was put on the cross is His Son. Men put Him on the cross and God put Him on the throne. Men cast Him out and heaven took Him in. Men made Him an accursed thing and God glorified Him (Acts 2:22-24; 32-36; 5:29-31). The resurrection of Jesus Christ from the dead is God's personal proof to you and to all men everywhere that this Jesus Christ is His Son.

Have you accepted Jesus Christ as your Saviour? Is this real with you? Are you sure of eternal life? Do not depend on your feelings. Accept His gift of eternal life and enjoy it. "He that hath the Son hath life; and he that hath not the Son of God hath not life." What a Saviour we have!

> **These things have I written unto you that believe on the name of the Son of God; that ye may know that ye have eternal life, and that ye may believe on the name of the Son of God (I John 5:13).**

A more accurate translation of the last phrase of this verse would be "even to you that believe on the name of the Son of God." There is no questioning of faith here, for it is written to those who have believed. These things have been written so that the believer might *know* that he has eternal life. This means to know in our experience. It does not refer simply to a mental knowledge but to an experiential knowledge in life.

The Gospel of John shows how we are to *receive* life. "But these are written, that ye might believe that Jesus is the Christ, the Son of God; and that believing ye might have life through His name" (John 20:31). The theme of the whole Gospel of John is in chapter 1:4, "In Him was life." Jesus says in John 5:26, "As the Father hath life in himself; so hath he given to the Son to have life in himself." As soon as a person accepts Jesus Christ, he has entered into relationship with the Son of God and he immediately has eternal life. *In Him is life.*

The Epistle of John was written so the believer may *know* that he has eternal life. May I review it again? In chapter 2 we know that we have eternal life because we keep His commandments. In chapter 3 we know that we have eternal life because we love the brethren. In chapter 5 we know that we have eternal life because we believe His Word. In chapter 5:20 we know we have eternal because we are in Him that is true.

My friend, if we do not *enjoy* the life we have in Christ, it is because of our unbelief. We still have doubts about the accomplishment of Christ on the cross. When Jesus Christ died on the cross, He finished a complete work. He was buried, but He was raised again from the dead, and He will never again be put on the cross. He will never again be a sacrifice for sin. "For Christ also hath ONCE suffered for sins, the just for the unjust" (I Pet. 3:18).

We are sanctified "through the offering of the body of Jesus Christ ONCE FOR ALL" (Heb. 10:10).

"This man, after He had offered *ONE* sacrifice for sins *FOR EVER,* sat down at the right hand of God" (Heb. 10:12).

"By ONE offering He hath perfected FOREVER them that are sanctified" (Heb. 10:14).

Christ will never die again. After a person has accepted the Saviour and received the atonement and been made a child of God and given eternal life, then if there is a possibility of being lost, such a person must be lost forever. There can be no more sacrifice for sin. Christ cannot be put back on the cross again.

Christ has accomplished a perfect, a complete work. We may fail because of our frailty. We may get out of the will of God by doing things we should not do or saying things we should not say. *This does not destroy eternal life.* It does affect our fellowship with God. It will have an affect on our service when we fail God. However, our failures never affect our relationship or our possession of life in Christ Jesus. After all, we do not keep ourselves in our relationship to Christ. Jesus prayed, "Holy Father, keep through thine own name those whom thou hast given me, that they may be one, as we are. While I was with them in the world, I kept them in thy name . . . I pray not that thou shouldest take them out of the world, but that thou shouldest keep them from the evil" (John17:11,12,15). You are kept by the power of God! (I Pet. 1:5). God has made Himself responsible for the keeping of every one of His true children.

CERTAINTY IN PRAYER

The absolute assurance of life will lead the Christian to assurance in prayer. Prayer is pouring out our heart to God. This can be done with confidence and boldness in Christ, coming into the very presence of God with our requests and knowing that God hears us.

> And this is the confidence that we have in him, that, if we ask any thing according to his will, he heareth us:
>
> And if we know that he hears us, whatsoever we ask, we know that we have the petitions that we desired of him (I John 5:14,15).

We can come to the throne of God with boldness because *we are confident about the future.* Scripture assures us of this. "Let us therefore come boldly unto the throne of grace" (Heb. 4:16).

"Abide in him; that, when he shall appear, we may have confidence, and not be ashamed before him at his coming" (I John 2:28).

"Herein is our love made perfect, that we may have boldness in the day of judgment" (I John 4:17).

We can have boldness before God also *in view of our present experience.* "If our heart condemn us not, then have we confidence toward God" (I John 3:21). "This is the confidence that we have in him, that, if we ask anything according to his will, he heareth us" (I John 5:14). This boldness is a present experience in coming to the throne of God and there obtaining mercy.

The consciousness of divine life brings the believer into a place of boldness. The more we realize our relationship to the living God, the more we realize that we are the children of One who is God, the more we see that His life has become our life, the deeper will be our appreciation of the fact that God's heart is wrapped up in us who are believers.

It is when we see the great yearning of His heart for our fellowship that we have boldness to come to God just like a child comes with confidence to father or mother. A child will not have that same confidence with strangers. Yet he will bring to the attention of the parents every small, insignificant, childish thing that comes into his life. A parent's loving heart listens and enters into his child's problems and cares and undertakes for him. So it is with our heavenly Father. God has made us the objects of His love and His grace. The consciousness of this relationship to the Son of God and the realization that we are partakers of divine life in Christ Jesus give us this boldness in His presence.

God gives to us this wonderful privilege of prayer. So much has been written and spoken about prayer, and yet we know so little about it. How much does it enter into our practical experience? How often do we come to God with our requests on the ground of our relationship to Him? Do we understand the conditions attached to prayer? It may be well to go over them briefly once more.

John 14:13,14 informs us that we should ask in the name of Jesus and that the purpose of our requests should be that the Father may be glorified in the Son. This rules out selfish requests for selfish motives. In John 15:7 Jesus declares union with Him to be a condition connected with prayer: "If ye abide in me, and my words abide in you, ye shall ask what ye will, and it shall be done unto you." When the Word of God is abiding in the believer, then that person is abiding in Christ. To abide is to live a life of obedience. The person who abides in the Word will get the mind of God, and then it will follow that those things will be requested in prayer which will bring glory to Him.

In John 16:23-27 Jesus tells his disciples that He will no longer make requests for them but that they are to go directly to the Father in the name of Jesus. The ground for the answer to prayer is not our love for the Father but it is His love for us. Jesus Himself made His request in John

17:24 on the basis of the Father's love for Him: " . . . for thou lovedst me before the foundation of the world." Jesus tells us in John 16 that on the ground of the Father's love for us, He will grant the request. Sometimes He will answer a request with a "No" because He knows what is the very best for us.

Finally, according to this verse in I John 5:14,15, prayer, to be answered, must be according to His will. What is His will? How can we know His will? How can we know whether we are praying in His will or in self will? The will of God is revealed to us in the Word of God. His purposes and plans and program are all in the Book.

I have noticed in my years of ministry that the first step in backsliding is neglect of the Word of God. How can you be obedient to the Word of God unless you read it? How can you know the will of God unless you abide in the Word of God? People come to me telling that the Lord showed them this or that. Ah, the question is, did this arise out of imagination and self-will, or did it come from the Word of God? It is certainly true that the Spirit of God takes the truths of the Word of God and makes them very real to us. He puts them into our hearts and reveals the will of God to us. Then, when we pray according to His will, He hears us.

This consciousness and realization of relationship to God and partnership with Him in His divine life bring the believer into a place of boldness in prayer. This is not to be belief only, but it is to be a daily experience! There is nothing too great for God to do for man, and there is nothing too small for God to grant to His people. "He that spared not his own Son, but delivered him up for us all, how shall he not with him also freely give us all things?" (Rom. 8:32). He numbers our steps (Job 14:16). The very hairs of our head are all numbered (Matt. 10:30). He bottles our tears (Psa. 56:8). "Are not two sparrows sold for a farthing? and one of them shall not fall on the ground without your Father . . . Fear ye not therefore, ye are of more value than many sparrows" (Matt. 10:29-31).

The Lord is desirous of doing more for us than we can ever ask or think. The problem is that self-will and sin enter in, and we try to come before God with unconfessed sin in our lives. Hence, we are not clean before God. He has revealed to us how to be cleansed in I John 1:9. If we confess our sin, He forgives us and cleanses us. Then we are to go on with God and walk in fellowship with Him. We will be taught to know His will, to know the things that please God, and our prayers will be in His will.

Sometimes God's people are actually amazed that God should answer their prayers because they really didn't expect them to be answered. An example of this is in Acts 12. The disciples were praying for the deliverance of Peter, and the Lord wonderfully answered their prayer. When Peter knocked on the door, they wouldn't believe that it was really Peter. Isn't it true that sometimes we pray so casually that ten minutes later we have forgotten what we prayed for? Yet the astounding fact is that God answers and meets our need. There is nothing that God will withhold from the one who prays, believing.

In Matthew 17 the disciples tried unsuccessfully to cast out a demon, and then they asked the Lord why they could not do it. Jesus answered, "Because of your unbelief: for verily I say unto you, If ye have faith as a grain of mustard seed, ye shall say unto this mountain, Remove hence to yonder place; and it shall remove; and nothing shall be impossible unto you. Howbeit this kind goeth not out but by prayer and fasting" (Matt. 17:20,21). In other words, He is offering to them a touch of omnipotence! He has given to His disciples a tool which is so powerful that there is not a force on the earth to equal it. Study the Bible and you will find examples in Genesis, Exodus, and Numbers where whole nations have been delivered from extinction by the prayers of one man.

The sad fact is that we Christians possess the most powerful weapon in the universe but we do not use it as we should. We preach about it and teach about it, but we do not use it. When we try to use it, we fail to use it properly. We fail to study the Scriptures to learn precisely what it does say about prayer. Then, because we do not get what we want, we doubt that God answers prayer.

The Word of God *commands* us to pray. "I exhort therefore, that, first of all, supplications, prayers, intercessions, and giving of thanks, be made for all men; For kings, and for all that are in authority; that we may lead a quiet and peaceable life in all godliness and honesty" (I Tim. 2:1,2). God has given into the hands of the Christians a tool whereby we may have peace, assurance, quietness in our land. Yet we live in a world and in a nation that is chaotic today. Why don't we use our weapon? Why don't we? I believe that if the Christians in America were to get down on their knees before God in the blessed ministry of prayer and intercession, there is nothing that God would hold back from us and from our nation. There is one problem. Do we really mean business with God?

Our Lord gave us a parable about that very thing. A man went to his friend in the middle of the night and wanted to borrow three loaves of bread, but the friend answered him, "I am in bed, my wife is in bed, my children are in bed, so I am not going to get up to give you three loaves of bread." The man replied, "Brother, the sooner you give me the three loaves, the sooner you can go back to bed." So he just kept on knocking and knocking. "I want my three loaves of bread." The Lord says that the friend will get up and give him as many loaves as he wants because of his "importunity"—because he really means business (Luke 11:5-10). Sometimes I wonder, do we really mean business with God when we pray? Or are we just saying words?

This boldness before God in prayer will also express itself in intercession. In fact, the more one spends time in the presence of God, the more one prays for others. We come now to two difficult verses about prayer for others.

> If any man see his brother sin a sin which is not
> unto death, he shall ask, and he shall give him life
> for them that sin not unto death. There is a sin
> unto death: I do not say that he shall pray for it.
>
> All unrighteousness is sin: and there is a sin not
> unto death (I John 5:16,17).

He is definitely talking about God's people here because he says, "If any man see his brother sin." I believe this reveals God in His governmental dealing with His people, His own family. Let us look more into the detail of these verses which have been a problem to so many of God's people.

This is not talking about the unpardonable sin as found in Matthew 12. That sin is ascribing to Satan those things which are done by the Spirit of God. Our Lord performed miracles under the power and anointing of the Holy Spirit, but the people of His day, especially the leaders, said that He did His miracles according to Beelzebub, the prince of the demons. "This fellow doth not cast out devils, but by Beelzebub the prince of the devils" (Matt. 12:24). To put it in very blunt language, they were saying that Jesus Christ came from hell. They said this after the Lord had already presented His credentials as the Messiah and after His gracious words had proceeded from His mouth. The Lord Jesus said that this sin was unpardonable.

Nor are these verses talking about the wilful sin of Hebrews 10. The wilful sin is the despising of the Person of Christ, the Spirit of Christ, and the Work of Christ. "For if we sin wilfully after that we have received the knowledge of the truth, there remaineth no more sacrifice for sins, But a certain fearful looking for of judgment and fiery indignation, which shall devour the adversaries. He that despised Moses' law died without mercy under two or three witnesses: Of how much sorer punishment, suppose ye, shall he be thought worthy, who hath TRODDEN UNDER FOOT THE SON OF GOD, and hath COUNTED THE

BLOOD OF THE COVENANT, wherewith he was santified, AN UNHOLY THING, and hath DONE DESPITE UNTO THE SPIRIT OF GRACE?" (Heb. 10:26-29). This is actually the end of the argument of the Book of Hebrews. If Christ is spurned as the Saviour, then there is nothing left but judgment. This is the wilful sin.

These verses in I John are talking about the fact that there are limitations in praying for others. There is a sin unto death and this sin may be committed by a believer. This sin might be a continuous wrong attitude before God. We are not to pray for it or even to make inquiry concerning it.

There is no question in my mind that God, in His governmental dealing with His people, sometimes permits physical death as a judgment upon a person so that his soul might be saved at the coming of the Lord.

I Corinthians tells of a young man who had committed adultery. Even before the man showed any repentance, the church was actually glorying in their liberty. Paul wrote that when they would come together, with his spirit and with the Spirit of the Lord Jesus Christ, they should "deliver such an one unto Satan for the destruction of the flesh, that the spirit may be saved in the day of the Lord Jesus" (I Cor. 5:5). In chapter five of Acts, Ananias and Sapphira came under the judgment of God and died physically. I believe this is what John refers to in this Epistle. The sin unto death is a sin which brings physical death as the judgment of God upon one of His children.

Scripture states three reasons for the physical death of a Christian:

1. A Christian may die because his work is finished. Paul could say, "The time of my departure is at hand. I have fought a good fight, I have finished my course, I have kept the faith" (II Tim. 4:6,7). Peter wrote, "Knowing that shortly I must put off this my tabernacle, even as our Lord Jesus Christ hath shewed me" (II Pet. 1:14). Their work was finished.

2. A Christian may die for the glory of God. Jesus told Peter that he would be martyred and that by his death he should glorify God (John 21:18,19). Numerous martyrs have died for the glory of God.

3. A Christian may die under the chastening hand of God. Paul had a recommendation for dealing with the man in the Corinthian congregation, the man who was living in adultery. He was to be delivered unto Satan for the destruction of the flesh so that his spirit might be saved (I Cor. 5:5). When Paul reprimands the Corinthians for their unbelief in regard to the Lord's Supper, he says, "For this cause many are weak and sickly among you, and many sleep" (I Cor. 11:30). In Acts 5, Ananias and Sapphira were chastened with physical death because of their lie. These verses in I John 5 are referring to Christians and speak of a "sin unto death."

I firmly believe it is possible for a Christian to die prematurely under the chastening hand of God. This does not indicate that such a Christian is lost eternally, but it does mean that such a person is robbed of the opportunity of staying on earth as a testimony for the glory of God. None of us wants to leave this world before his work is completed. Yet, Scripture teaches that some Christians die under the chastening hand of God.

This is a fitting time for a word of warning. Let us each evaluate his own life and not judge each other. It is not your prerogative, nor mine, to conclude that a certain individual has died or is dying under the judgment of God. Let us leave that judgment completely in the hands of God. The Lord has never told us that we should be the judge or the jury! However, it is well for us to ponder this matter of God's governmental dealing with His own people. This thought should encourage us to be walking continually with our actions, our words, and our whole life in its very attitude, all for the glory of God.

We see in verse 16 that there is a sin unto death and there is a sin which is not unto death. Everything that is not righteous is sin. All lawlessness and every transgression of the law is sin. We Christians ought to be very, very conscious of our relationship with each other. The very fact that a fellow Christian is sinning should stimulate us to intercessory prayer. We are to be bold in prayer for one another. Yet we are told there is a sin unto death, and God alone is the judge of this. This sobering fact should cause us to take our place before God, humbly walk with Him, and let Him work out His perfect will in us.

CERTAINTY OF VICTORY

We know that whosoever is born of God sinneth not; but he that is begotten of God keepeth himself, and that wicked one toucheth him not.

And we know that we are of God, and the whole world lieth in wickedness.

And we know that the Son of God is come, and hath given us an understanding, that we may know him that is true, and we are in him that is true, even in his Son Jesus Christ. This is the true God, and eternal life (I John 5:18-20).

There are three divine certainties of victory:
1. The assurance of holiness in verse 18,
2. The assurance of life in verse 19,
3. The assurance of redemption in verse 20.

1. The Assurance of Holiness

"We know that whosoever is born of God sinneth not." We shall not go into a full discussion of chapter 3:6-8 again. However, we must face sin realistically. Whatever is unrighteous is sin, and a Christian is in a body that is not yet glorified. Christians do sin. There would be no need for I John 1:9 if this were not so.

However, that which is born of God cannot sin. The new man in Christ is created in righteousness and true holiness

(Eph. 4:24). A man in Christ is a new creature (II Cor. 5:17). When we accepted Jesus as our Saviour, we were made new creatures in Christ and received the Spirit of God to indwell us. That new man cannot sin because it is born of God. God is righteous, and that which is born of God cannot sin, nor can the wicked one touch that which is begotten of God.

The Christian, then, is a person who is still in the body with its frailty and its desires but who has also become a new person, begotten of God and indwelt by the Spirit of God. According to Romans 6:11, the Christian is to live his life reckoning himself to be dead to sin but alive to God through Jesus Christ, our Lord. Therefore, the Christian life should no longer be characterized or dominated by sin.

If your life is dominated by sin and you profess to be a Christian, then examine yourself to see whether you are really in the faith. There are a great many people who profess they believe in the Saviour, but who have never had any relationship with Christ. They may belong to a church and assent to all the historical facts of Christ's death, burial, and resurrection and yet not have a real experience of accepting the Saviour. If you have had a personal relationship with the Saviour, your life will not be characterized and dominated by sin. There will be in you that which is born of God, and the Spirit of God will keep you from the evil one because "that wicked one toucheth him not."

God has given us this assurance of holiness in our lives. God has made the provision for restoration so that if our fellowship with the Lord is broken by sin, we are forgiven and cleansed as soon as we confess that sin.

2. The Assurance of Life

"We know that we are of God." Knowing we are of God gives us assurance of life. There are many other Scriptures which give us this same assurance.

We "are kept by the power of God through faith unto salvation ready to be revealed in the last time" (I Pet. 1:5).

"I know whom I have believed, and am persuaded that he is able to keep that which I have committed unto him against that day" (II Tim. 1:12).

"Being confident of this very thing, that he which hath begun a good work in you will perform it until the day of Jesus Christ" (Phil 1:6).

"Now unto him that is able to keep you from falling, and to present you faultless before the presence of his glory with exceeding joy, to the only wise God our Saviour . . . " (Jude 24).

"I pray God your whole spirit and soul and body be preserved blameless unto the coming of our Lord Jesus Christ. Faithful is he that calleth you, who also will do it" (I Thess. 5:23,24).

"Holy Father, keep through thine own name those whom thou hast given me" (John 17:11).

" . . . Looking unto Jesus, the author and finisher of our faith" (Heb. 12:2).

We are of God. The whole world lieth in the lap of the wicked one. There is a clear cut distinction stated here. The world is in the opposite camp. This was the theme of Peter's sermon in Acts 2 when he said, "You crucified Him but God raised Him; you cast Him out but God took him in. You are in the wrong camp!"

This life-giving relationship is an individual, personal matter. Can you say that you are a child of God, that you are of God? Do you have a relationship with God through His Son, Jesus Christ? If you do not, you can come into such a relationship right now by accepting Jesus Christ as your own, personal Saviour.

3. The Assurance of Redemption

Verse 20 assures us of our redemption because "we are in him." We know that the Son of God has come, and we have an understanding of the reason for His coming. "For the Son of man is come to seek and to save that which was lost" (Luke 19:10). "This is a faithful saying, and worthy of all acceptation, that Christ Jesus came into the world to save sinners; of whom I am chief" (I Tim. 1:15).

"We may know him that is true" both by faith and by our experience. We know that He is the true Saviour, the only Saviour, the Saviour who guarantees salvation by His own resurrection from the dead. It also states that "we are in him that is true." We are in union with Him by faith.

"THIS is the true God, and eternal life." This! This Jesus Christ!

"I am the door: by me if any man enter in, he shall be saved" (John 10:9).

"I am the light of the world: he that followeth me shall not walk in darkness, but shall have the light of life" (John 8:12).

"I am the living bread which came down from heaven: if any man eat of this bread, he shall live for ever" (John 6:51).

"Father, the hour is come; glorify thy Son, that thy Son also may glorify thee: As thou hast given him power over all flesh, that he should give eternal life to as many as thou hast given him. And this is life eternal, that they might know thee the true God, and Jesus Christ, whom thou hast sent" (John 17:1-3).

THE
CONCLUSION

Little children, keep yourselves from idols. Amen (I John 5:21).

The conclusion is an appeal. It is an appeal to God's people to keep themselves from idols. An idol is anything that comes between us and our heart affection for the Saviour. Covetousness is idolatry (Eph. 5:5). He has just said in verse 20 that we know the Son of God is true, that we are in the Son of God who is true, and that this Son of God is the true God and eternal life. Now comes the solemn warning about idols.

Is there anything or anybody that takes the place of Christ in your heart? In your devotion? Do you have any ambitions which displace Him in your heart?

The very first verse in the Bible says, "In the beginning God." If Dr. Westcott, the eminent Bible scholar, is correct, then the last verse of the Bible to be written is: "Keep yourselves from idols." The whole Bible between the first verse and this last verse reveals in type, in shadow, in experience, in reality that the heart of God is displayed to us in the person of the Lord Jesus Christ. *He is the true God and eternal life.*

He is the *way* to the Father (John 14:6).

He is the *truth* that sets us free (John 8:31-32 and John 14:6).

He is the *life* that brings us into relationship with the living God (John 14:6).

REVIEW
OF THE
EPISTLE

The Bible was written for us to know the purpose of God and His desire and His love for us. Not only does it reveal that He redeems sinners and makes them His children, but also that He greatly longs for the fellowship of His children. So let us review this Epistle in an attempt to catch the movement of the Spirit of God in giving it to us.

.In the Gospel of John we are taught how to receive life by faith in Christ. In the Epistle of John we are taught how to enjoy that life. In the Gospel of John we learn that we receive eternal life by faith. In the Epistle of John we know that we have eternal life because we experience it.

The entire Epistle of John deals with our fellowship with God. There is given to us a three-fold revelation of God in this Epistle:

We have fellowship with God who is light, that is, who is holy.

We have fellowship with God who is righteous.

We have fellowship with God who is love.

I John 1:1-4 is the introduction. This states the experience of John and the other apostles and gives their testimony. The subject is the Lord Jesus Christ, the Incarnate Word of God. The purpose of the coming of our Lord was to redeem a people for His name and to make these redeemed ones fit for fellowship with God. The apostles told what they had seen, heard, and experienced so that we might have fellowship with the Father and with the Son and that through such fellowship our joy might be filled full.

I John 1:5–2:28 discusses fellowship with God *who is light.* The *test* of such fellowship is walking in the light (1:5-8). The *provision* for the fellowship is the confession of our sins (1:9-10). The *ground* for the fellowship is the complete work of Christ at the cross and His advocacy on the basis of His abiding propitiation for our sin (2:1,2). The *evidence* of such fellowship is obedience to His Word, submission to His will, and love for the brethren (2:3-11). This provides a way in which we can test whether or not we are in fellowship with God. It is also the way others may know whether or not we are in fellowship with God.

The *place* of the fellowship is in the family of God (2:12-28). There is no admonition to the fathers in the family because they are mature Christians. The young men in the family have had victory over the devil, but now they have a new enemy, the world. The babes in Christ are exhorted against false teachers, those who deny the Incarnate Word of God. This division of the Epistle closes with an appeal to all the family to abide in Him.

I John 2:29–4:6 discusses fellowship with God *who is righteous.* The fact that God is righteous is stated in 2:29 and 3:7. This naturally raises the question, "How can I have fellowship with God who is righteous when I do so many unrighteous things?"

We are *encouraged* in fellowship with a righteous God because of our relationship to Him (3:1-3). We do not belong to this world but we are His beloved children, even though we are in frailty. Our *present experience* is relationship. We are the children of God. Our *future experience* will be that we shall be like Him when He comes. Everyone who has this hope will purify himself, even as He is pure. This is our *present experience* of purification on the basis of our hope.

The *opposition* to the fellowship comes from satanic forces. The children of God are contrasted with the children of the devil (3:4-13). Righteousness characterizes the people of God, whereas wickedness and sinfulness are manifest in those who do not belong to God. The unsaved man lives a life which is characterized by sin. The child of God lives a life in his thoughts, words, and deeds which is not dominated nor characterized by sin.

The *evidence* of such fellowship with God is love for the brethren, confidence in prayer, and obedience to His Word (3:14-24). We have that wonderful confidence before God when our hearts do not condemn us and there is nothing between us and the Lord. Then we come knowing that He hears us and will meet our need and answer our prayer to glorify Himself in us. He explains that His commandments for us are that we should believe on the name of the Son of God and that we should love one another as He gave us command. We know that we belong to Him by the indwelling Spirit which He has given to us.

The Spirit of Christ and the spirit of antichrist are contrasted (4:1-6). We are to try the spirits. Anyone who denies the Incarnate Word of God, who denies that Jesus Christ is God manifest in the flesh, is not of God.

I John 4:7—5:5 discusses fellowship with God *who is love.* The *revelation* that God is love is given in verses 7-10. This love was demonstrated to us and for us at the cross. Our fellowship with this God who is love is manifested by our love to others, especially to those who are the people of God. As we walk with Him, fear is gone because perfect love casts out fear.

After we are told to love the brethren, the natural question is, "Who are my brethren?" This is answered in the first five verses of chapter 5. My brother is anyone who confesses that Jesus is the Christ, the Son of God.

The Epistle continues by encouraging us. We have victory over the world, and this victory is guaranteed to us because of our union with the Son of God Himself. Then we are given the certainty of God's testimony concerning all the things which He has done for us. We have the certainty of life eternal because we are in the Son of God (5:9-13). Not to believe that we have eternal life in the Son of God is to make God a liar. God has born testimony to the fact that everyone who puts his trust in Jesus *has* eternal life. This certainty of eternal life gives to us a confidence in prayer (5:14-17).

The Epistle concludes with the certainty of victory. We may have confidence in the presence of God. We may have confidence in a life that is not characterized by sin. We may have confidence in a life that is not under the authority of Satan. We know that we belong to God. We know Him that is true and we are in Him that is true, that is, Jesus Christ. We want Him to be the very center of our lives.

Then there is the final plea. My little children, keep yourselves from idols. Make Christ the very center of your life!

May the Lord bless you as you read and reread this wonderful Epistle of John. The Lord bless you for His name's sake.

THE
SECOND
EPISTLE
OF JOHN

During John's lifetime there were certain false teachers who had come into the church of Christ and they were declaring that Jesus Christ was a mere man. They were not standing for the truth and were denying that Jesus is God manifest in the flesh. The Gnostic heresy declared that since all matter and all flesh are evil and God is holy, therefore a holy God cannot dwell with that which is evil. Hence they said that Jesus Christ cannot be God but is a created being, possibly an emanation from God—higher than the angels, but still a created being. John refutes this heresy in his Epistles.

May I say that if Jesus Christ is not who He claimed to be, God manifest in the flesh, the El Shaddai whom Abraham worshipped, then all the truth of the gospel is void. Then His work on the cross is of no redeeming value, and there is no resurrection from the dead. When Jesus Christ is not worshipped as God or when He ceases to be the center of our worship, then we no longer have a Christian fellowship.

In the First Epistle John speaks of the *nature* and the *place* of the fellowship and how we know that we are saved in Christ Jesus. In the Second Epistle he deals with the *limit* of the fellowship, that is, whom to *exclude* from the fellowship of God's people. In the Third Epistle John talks about the *extent* of the fellowship, that is, whom to *include* in the fellowship. In the Second Epistle He condemns heresy because of departure from the truth and from the love of the truth. In the Third Epistle the apostle condems divisions and schisms among God's people.

The key of the Second Epistle of John is: *Walking in the Truth.*

THE SALUTATION

The elder unto the elect lady and her children, whom I love in the truth; and not I only, but also all they that have known the truth;

For the truth's sake, which dwelleth in us, and shall be with us for ever.

Grace be with you, mercy, and peace, from God the Father, and from the Lord Jesus Christ, the Son of the Father, in truth and love.

I rejoiced greatly that I found of thy children walking in truth, as we have received a commandment from the Father (II John 1-4).

Jesus said, "I am the way, the truth, and the life" (John 14:6). Colossians 2:3 tells us that in Christ Jesus God has hidden all the treasures of wisdom and knowledge. We are not searching for the truth. *Jesus Christ is the truth.* We may not understand all about it. We may not have experienced much of it. This does not alter the fact that Jesus Christ is the truth. This is the very foundation of Christianity.

Notice that the apostle mentions the truth in each of the first four verses: "Whom I love in the truth," "all they that have known the truth," "for the truth's sake," "in truth and love," "walking in truth." Walking in the truth is the activity of one who loves the truth. In other words, what we believe will be manifest in how we live. If we believe that Jesus Christ is the eternal Son of God, and if we love Him, this will affect our entire life. It will especially affect our attitude to those who are related to Him, those who are fellow members in the family of God. We will love the people of God because we love the truth. Christ·is the truth.

I cannot repeat it too often. The great foundation for fellowship is the person of Christ. When Christ ceases to be the center of fellowship, then divisions and heresies come in. Those who do not love the truth, who are not related to the Saviour, will enter the fellowship and cause trouble. The end result will be a worldly church. Such a church will include those who detract from the person of Christ. Such people become the instruments of Satan for the destruction of the fellowship.

We are dealing with very practical matters. Where there is no love for the truth, there will be little love for God's people. John here is appealing for a genuine love for the Saviour, a genuine love for the truth, a genuine love for the Incarnate Word of God. This was the very heart of the doctrine of the early church. It is also the very heart of fellowship. If only we would follow this truth today! Then Jesus Christ would be the center of our worship, and we would include all those who believe the truth.

EXHORTATION TO LOVE AND OBEDIENCE

And now I beseech thee, lady, not as though I wrote a new commandment unto thee, but that which we had from the beginning, that we love one another.

And this is love, that we walk after his commandments. This is the commandment, That, as ye have heard from the beginning, ye should walk in it (II John 5,6).

We are admonished to love one another in the truth. This theme runs through all the Epistle of John. God sees our faith but men experience our love. The manifestation of our love is obedience to His commandments.

Jesus said the same thing: "He that hath my commandments, and keepeth them, he it is that loveth me" (John 14:21). "If a man love me, he will keep my words" (John 14:23). The whole New Testament declares that the manifestation before the world that we love the Saviour is our obedience to His Word. Love is the motive for that obedience. "But that the world may know that I love the Father; and as the Father gave me commandment, even so I do." (John 14:31).

WARNING AGAINST ERROR

For many deceivers are entered into the world, who confess not that Jesus Christ is come in the flesh. This is a deceiver and an antichrist.

Look to yourselves, that we lose not those things which we have wrought, but that we receive a full reward.

Whosoever transgresseth, and abideth not in the doctrine of Christ, hath not God. He that abideth in the doctrine of Christ, he hath both the Father and the Son.

If there come any unto you, and bring not this doctrine, receive him not into your house, neither bid him God speed:

For he that biddeth him God speed is partaker of his evil deeds (II John 7—11).

John here speaks very emphatically concerning those who deny that Jesus Christ is God manifest in the flesh. He calls them deceivers and declares that they are to be excluded from our fellowship. The danger is that we may become lax in our relationships and permit those who deny the Incarnate Word of God to enter into our fellowship. If we do this, we are in danger of losing our reward. So there is a necessity to be separated from such deceivers.

Does John mean that if someone who denies the Incarnate Word of God comes into the church, he should not be received? That is exactly what he is saying. We who believe in Him cannot have fellowship with one who denies the Son of God, denies His Word, His work on the cross, His resurrection. John says clearly that if we receive him, or bid him God speed, we are partakers of his evil deeds. There must be separation of believers from those who deny the deity of our Lord Jesus Christ.

PERSONAL REMARKS

Having many things to write unto you, I would not write with paper and ink: but I trust to come unto you, and speak face to face, that our joy may be full.

The children of thy elect sister greet thee. Amen. (II John 12,13).

There is great joy in fellowship with those who love the Saviour. This enjoyment of fellowship is something that is outside the understanding and experience of the man of the world. There is a very special bond between those who really know and love the One who came into the world and gave Himself for us.

I have travelled in many parts of the world and have been in homes in many countries. Always there is a feeling of oneness with those who know my Lord. There is a fulness of joy in speaking face to face with fellow believers. Several times in his Gospel and also in his Epistles John speaks of fulness of joy. This is one of them. "I trust to come unto you, and speak face to face, that our joy may be full."

"Then they that feared the LORD spake often one to another: and the LORD hearkened, and heard it, and a book of remembrance was written before him for them that feared the LORD, and that thought upon his name" (Mal. 3:16). I trust that you and I may know this joy.

THE
THIRD
EPISTLE
OF JOHN

This Epistle gives the *extent* of the fellowship by telling whom to *include* in the fellowship. It condemns divisions and schisms by those who have departed from the love of the truth.

The theme of III John is: *Love in the Truth.* This Epistle is talking about loving those who are in the truth. It recommends that all those who are brethren should stand for the truth.

WALKING IN THE TRUTH

The elder unto the wellbeloved Gaius, whom I love in the truth.

Beloved, I wish above all things that thou mayest prosper and be in health, even as thy soul prospereth.

For I rejoiced greatly, when the brethren came and testified of the truth that is in thee, even as thou walkest in the truth.

I have no greater joy than to hear that my children walk in truth (III John 1-4).

1. His Desire for Gaius (vv. 1 and 2)

You will notice that John has a warm heart, filled with the Spirit of God, in his great desire for God's people to know something of fellowshiping together in the truth. People from all over the world have so many different philosophies that some may wonder who is telling the truth. How wonderful to *know* that Jesus Christ is the embodiment not only of love but also of truth!

John, being in love with the Saviour, is in love with God's people. I take it from this verse that Gaius was revelling in the truth of God but that he had a frail body. John wishes that he might prosper and be in health in body just as his soul prospers. I am afraid that today it is often just the other way around. We are very much exercised about how our bodies prosper; we become health faddists, food faddists, sun worshipers, concerned that our bodies be beautiful and healthy. How much are we concerned about our health in our relation to Christ? We become very concerned when we do not feel too well. Are we as much concerned when our hearts grow cold towards Christ?

Do you realize that the great majority of professing Christians never grow, never mature? They may be professing Christians for years and yet know little about the Saviour in practical life. They know so little about the reality of life in Christ, about the purposes of God and His will and His desire. They do not know God's program. Where can God's program be found? *In the Bible.* Oh, how I like what John says here: "Gaius, I'd like for you to prosper in your body just as you are prospering in your soul."

2. The Character of Gaius (verse 3)

The life of Gaius was characterized by walking in the truth. John rejoices in this, and other brethren bore testimony to the fact that Gaius walked in the truth. Not only did he believe the truth, but he lived the truth, and the truth lived in him. He was in love with the Saviour, and his whole life was a manifestation of the fact that he was living in fellowship with the Lord. Walking in the truth is one of the great evidences of a heart in fellowship with God.

This man walked in the truth, and he had a real testimony for God. The brethren testified to that. You see, loving the truth makes one spiritually healthy, and service will be the natural outflow of a walk with God. When we try to put it the other way around, putting service before our walk with God, we soon get tired of service and our work becomes legalistic. It no longer brings joy to the heart, but it becomes a burden. Unfortunately, there are a great many people who endure religion instead of enjoying Christ! I hope you may know something of the joy and blessing and wonder of knowing the Saviour. May you be strong in spirit as this man Gaius was.

3. *John's Rejoicing* (verse 4)

It is a real joy for a pastor or a Bible teacher or a Sunday School teacher, or a friend, or a parent, to lead someone to Christ and to see him hungry for the Word of God. It is a thrill to go to a Bible conference and see hundreds of people who are using their vacation time to attend Bible studies, morning, afternoon, and evening. The world knows nothing about this wonderful hunger for the Word of God.

It rejoices my heart, too, to see people walking in the truth. I love to see young people carry their Bibles and read them whenever they have a chance. How I rejoice whenever I see real love for the Saviour!

WITNESSING TO THE TRUTH

Beloved, thou doest faithfully whatsoever thou doest to the brethren, and to strangers;

> Which have borne witness of thy charity before the church:. whom if thou bring forward on, their journey after a godly sort, thou shalt do well:
>
> Because that for his name's sake they went forth, taking nothing of the Gentiles.
>
> We therefore ought to receive such, that we might be fellow-helpers to the truth (III John 5-8).

Love for the people of God will be manifested in Christian courtesy and Christian hospitality and in encouraging other believers to bear testimony. Apparently there were those brethren who travelled from place to place, preaching the Word of God. Gaius took them in, cared for them, manifesting his love for God's people because of his love for the Saviour. These brethren would take nothing from the Gentile world but were trusting the Lord to meet their needs. John says that such ones should be received into the fellowship so that we may be fellow-helpers to the truth.

We are to take in and care for those who have sacrificed for the sake of the gospel. We are to receive such, that we might be fellow-helpers to the truth. We become coworkers with them. We are workers together with God (II Cor. 6:1 and I Cor. 3:9). We are workers together with each other.

My friend, God will never be in your debt. We are all on God's team. Each person is gifted to do a particular job, and some are told to go, some are told to stay. But we are all fellow-helpers to the truth, and when God rewards His people, we will all share in the reward. Some of us give all our time and strength to the study and the preaching of the Word. Others pray for us and help support us, but they also are to be giving this message of the truth to their friends. One of the greatest of all needs today is for God's people to pray for His servants everywhere as they minister the Word of God and also to pray for each other. We are all workers together, fellow-helpers to the truth.

THE WARNING

I wrote unto the church: but Diotrephes, who loveth to have the preeminence among them, receiveth us not.

Wherefore, if I come, I will remember his deeds which he doeth, prating against us with malicious words: and not content therewith, neither doth he himself receive the brethren, and forbiddeth them that would, and casteth them out of the church.

Beloved, follow not that which is evil, but that which is good. He that doeth good is of God: but he that doeth evil hath not seen God (III John 9-11).

In contrast to Gaius, this man Diotrephes, possibly a member of the same church, wanted the place of prominence. Even when someone who really loved the Lord came to the assembly and the brethren wanted to receive him, this man would forbid them to receive him. He wanted to dominate everything so he would cast others out.

Unfortunately, there are such men in churches today. They want to run everything and rule over everything. Such do not have time to manifest love or compassion for the babes in Christ. They are primarily concerned with their own position.

The people of God in an assembly are knitted together for a purpose. That purpose is worship, thanksgiving and praise to God, and then the feeding and encouragement of God's people. We are to manifest Christian grace and love and hospitality to each other. Especially are we to encourage those babes in Christ so they will be fed the Word of God and not be tossed about by every wind of doctrine. We should thank the Lord when He has sent a leader to us. The Lord has a place for every one of us. There are no two of us alike and we each have our gift. We are all a part of the body of Christ and members in particular, having a particular job, and each of us is to manifest love. (I Cor. 12:12–13:1).

When a stranger who really loves the Lord comes to our assembly, we need to recognize and manifest the fact that we have the same Saviour, the same hope, the same love in Christ Jesus. If there is a need, we should meet that need. I fear we have chased many dear people of God away from our churches because some of God's people want the place of prominence.

He warns us in verse 11 not to follow that which is evil, but to follow that which is good.

CONCLUSION AND PERSONAL GREETINGS

Demetrius hath good report of all men, and of the truth itself: yea, and we also bear record; and ye know that our record is true.

I had many things to write, but I wifl not with ink and pen write unto thee:

But I trust I shall shortly see thee, and we shall speak face to face. Peace be to thee. Our friends salute thee. Greet the friends by name (III John 12-14).

We now meet the third man in the Epistle, Demetrius, who has a good report and walks in the truth. In the assembly there is Gaius, who is weak in body but receives the brethren in the Lord. There is also Diotrephes, who "wants to be the big cheese," and he is opposed to every one who does not agree with him. Now John is saying that a stranger is coming to them and that John's record of him is good. He has a good report and knows the truth and walks in the truth. John's letter is written so that they will receive Demetrius.

The Second Epistle was to instruct them *not to* receive those who deny the Incarnate Word of God. The Third Epistle was to instruct them *to* receive those who have a good record and love the truth and walk in the truth.

The personal salutations are similar to the previous Epistle. I would love to see you face to face. I would love to talk with you about the things of the Lord. I am coming soon, I hope, and I am looking forward to our fellowship in the Saviour. **Give my friends my love.**

We can just see the friendliness of this man John to the people of God. No wonder he is called the Apostle of Love! Our Saviour is love personified. The Saviour so filled the heart of John with His divine love that John expressed it continually.

God grant that we will be numbered among those who walk in the truth and who love the brethren. May the Lord bless you for **His** name's sake!